The Agony of Decision

July, 2017

Karen,

Hope you're well and that you find this book helpful.

Best,

Logos Institute Best Practices Series

The Logos Institute for Crisis Management and Executive Leadership stands at the intersection of scholarship and practice, providing both rigorous analysis and practical application of key leadership principles. We illuminate best practices, current trends, emerging issues, and leadership skills.

The Logos Institute is a thought leader in its field, conducting research, publishing, and providing an extensive range of executive education workshops, seminars, conferences, and highly-customized coaching for senior executives of all sectors and around the world.

The Logos Institute creates and maintains an inventory of Best Practices, along with attendant tools and concepts that can inform our clients of what works and why, and that can help our clients to enhance their capacity to perform at higher and higher levels.

We harness and publish these best practices in a number of ways, from full-length books published by major publishing houses to chapters of or forewords to books, to articles in peer-reviewed scholarly and management journals, to contributions to mainstream media, social media, and blogs. We also publish highly distilled checklists on dozens of high-stakes decision-making, communication, or crisis-related situations.

The *Logos Institute Best Practices Series* provides conceptual frameworks that help to make sense of complicated issues, combined with case studies, examples, and actionable tools, tips, and techniques that help leaders make smart choices and build competitive advantage in high-stakes situations.

About Our People

We are a team of seasoned professionals passionately committed to serving our clients. We have extensive expertise as consultants, speakers, authors, professors, communicators, facilitators, managers, attorneys, entrepreneurs and executive coaches. We illuminate solutions to complex business challenges using a unique interdisciplinary framework and a distinctive approach. We cultivate individual and organizational strengths for maximum leadership development, especially in times of crisis and change. We help transform ideas, experience, and insight into innovation that matters.

We also teach in graduate business, law, and related programs, where we have an opportunity to test our conceptual work with the rigor required of highly-regarded educational institutions.

Each of our fellows is affiliated with one or more graduate institutions. Some of us have one or more formal faculty appointments. All of us teach via Logos Institute at universities that contract with us.

Learn more at www.logosconsulting.net or reach us at:

Logos Institute for Crisis Management and Executive Leadership
875 Avenue of the Americas, Suite 2300
New York, NY 10001

Other Books by Helio Fred Garcia

The Power of Communication: Skills to Build Trust, Inspire Loyalty, and Lead Effectively, FT Press/Pearson, 2012. Chinese Edition, Pearson Education Asia Ltd., Hong Kong, and Publishing House of Information Industry, Beijing, 2014.

Reputation Management: The Key to Successful Public Relations and Corporate Communication by John Doorley and Helio Fred Garcia, Routledge, Taylor & Francis Group, third edition, 2015; Korean edition, Alma Publishing, 2016; Chinese edition, Tsinghua University Press, pending, 2017. French edition pending, 2017. (First edition, 2007, second edition, 2011.)

Crisis Communications, two volumes, AAAA press, 1998, currently out of print.

Helio Fred Garcia

"Our goal is not to make up anyone's mind,

but rather to open minds;

to make the agony of decision so intense

that we can escape only by thinking."

-- Fred Friendly, former President of *CBS News*

and Dean of Columbia Journalism School

The Agony of Decision:

Mental Readiness and Leadership in a Crisis

By Helio Fred Garcia

Logos Institute Best Practices Series
Logos Institute for Crisis Management and Executive Leadership Press

Dedication

This book is dedicated to the thousands of clients and students
around the world who have trusted me with their reputations
and their professional development since 1980.

Thank you.

<u>Contents</u>

Acknowledgments

This book is the culmination of decades of observation, learning from mistakes, formal study, note-taking, counseling, lesson planning, teaching, speaking, and listening.

Since 2004 the Logos Institute for Crisis Management and Executive Leadership, which I have the honor to lead, has been studying patterns of effective and ineffective crisis response. We maintain an inventory of best practices, tools, techniques, and case studies that help clients better understand, and therefore better manage, the dynamics of a crisis.

This book would not have been possible without the help and work of current and past Logos Institute colleagues. In alphabetical order, they include: Evan Chethik, Michelle Cioffoletti, Anthony Ewing, Katie Garcia, Barbara Greene, Laurel Hart, Holly Helstrom, Elizabeth Jacques, Kristin Johnson, Raleigh Mayer, Adam Tiouririne, Oxana Trush, and Iris Wenting Xue. I thank them for their thoughtfulness, hard work, dedication to clients and students, and especially for their friendship.

Much of the material in this book was field tested with clients suffering real crises. Some of those have been my clients for decades. Contractually, I am not permitted to name most of them, but they know who they are. To them and all clients I say simply: Thank you for the trust you put in us, and for your support over the years.

As one finds in the Talmud, "I have learned much from my teachers; and from my colleagues more than from my teachers; but from my students more than from them all."

I have had the honor to serve on the New York University faculty since 1988. As this book goes to press, in the Summer of 2017, I am in the process of teaching my 104th NYU course. I thank the thousands of NYU students who have trusted me to facilitate their learning and professional development. One of the joys of teaching is how many of those students over the years have remained in touch; the dozens who have joined the NYU faculty to continue to pass along their own knowledge to new generations of students. And especially those who have joined the Logos Institute.

I have also been on the faculties of other universities in California, Switzerland, and China. Through Logos Institute contracts I have taught at yet other universities and specialized professional schools in the U.S., including a number affiliated with the U.S. armed forces. Although I do not get the chance to get to know the students in these programs as well as I would like, I am very grateful for the opportunity to work with them.

To all my students, thank you. Thank you for helping me to learn from you, individually and collectively. Many of you will recognize much of what appears in this book. I also want to thank the administrators and professors at all these schools who have supported my teaching in their schools, and who have encouraged me to keep finding new ways to think about and explain crises.

I also want to take a moment to thank my mentor and dear friend, America's Crisis Guru Jim Lukaszewski. More than 30 years ago I saw Jim at a public event, and was blown away. I met him for coffee and asked him to help me get into the crisis field for real. He said he'd keep an eye on me, and if he saw promise he'd do what he could. He has been a generous mentor, friend, and colleague ever since. However far I can see, it's because I stand on his shoulders. Thank you, Jim.

And finally, I want to thank my wife, Laurel Colvin, whom I met on the same day I received formal notice that I was appointed to the NYU faculty. What a good day that was! She is the love of my life and I'm honored to share my journey with her. And our two kids, Katie and Juliana Garcia. They are remarkable young women who make us proud every day.

Preface

In early 1987 I was a managing director in Adams & Rinehart, a leading public relations firm serving financial clients (now a part of Ogilvy Public Relations). I got a call from the head of the commercial paper department of Salomon Brothers, then a powerhouse investment bank and my largest client.

The challenge: Salomon Brothers was about to change the way commercial paper was traded. Commercial paper is a short-term loan that companies use to manage day-to-day cash flow. Those loans are traded actively among Wall Street firms. At the time, after each trade messengers would carry the physical loan documents around lower Manhattan, picking them up from Wall Street firms that sold and dropping them off at firms that bought the securities. It was wildly inefficient, but it was how securities were traded then. Salomon was about to launch the first-ever electronic trading of such securities. The result: faster, cheaper, and more accurate transactions. And no more paper. This was a potentially disruptive technology with the capacity to shake up old Wall Street ways; it was a proof-of-concept of moving to electronic trading of all securities.

My team and I went right to work, meeting with the client, organizing a press conference, training the people who would speak at it, and writing the materials that would be distributed to the press. And the press conference was a huge success.

The *New York Times*, *Wall Street Journal*, *Financial Times*, *Associated Press*, and *BusinessWeek* all covered it. The next day the headlines screamed about a revolution in securities trading. It was front page news not only in New York but also in London, Tokyo, Frankfurt, Sydney, and even in Rome.

That morning I was asked to meet with Salomon Brothers' head of PR. I thought I was there for a victory lap. Instead I got a scolding. "How dare you do this press conference!" Until then there had been no need to coordinate in advance, in keeping with the rough-and-tumble culture of the firm. That morning all the major media had put the firm's move into electronic trading on the front page, presumably a very positive outcome. But the very success of the press conference meant that those media were unlikely to give Salomon such positive coverage again for a long time. And Salomon was about to announce something genuinely big; something that would make a major difference in Salomon's strategic direction. But now, however important this may be, the media would be unlikely to cover it. They had already done their Salomon story.

So a relatively low-priority story, however dramatic, overtook a very important story. In other words, an excellently executed PR program prevented the client from attaining meaningful competitive advantage the way it had hoped. The client was furious. And rightly so. She wanted those front pages for the bigger story. And I had stolen them.

But the PR firm was ecstatic. My boss loved the press coverage, and arranged for me to receive that year's award, named for the PR firm's founder, for the best media relations execution. Thirty years later the Mel Adams Media Placement Award still hangs on my office wall, featuring the headlines from all over the world embedded behind glass. But I still feel somewhat conflicted about it.

Why This Book

I have been professionally involved in crisis and other high-stakes situations in one way or another since 1980; pretty much full-time in crisis and executive leadership since 1987. In the 1980s I worked at some of the biggest PR firms (Edelman, Burson-Marsteller, Ogilvy, and what is now called Weber Shandwick). And I also worked in-house as head of communication at a large investment bank and at a large accounting firm. And for 12 years – through the 1990s – I ran the crisis practice of a leading strategic communication firm that was part of The Omnicom Group. I loved working in each of those places. And I learned a lot.

But something was missing. One of the things I found in both the PR firms and the big companies was that crises generally provoked lots of activity, lots of tactical implementation of communication, and lots of missteps. And I was guilty of all of that.

Over the years I discovered that the real value in resolving crises is not in excellent internal and external communication, nor in highest-quality tactical execution, however important they may be – and they are mighty important.

Rather, real value came from helping clients figure out and answer the bigger questions and then make the tough choices in a timely way. The execution would follow. So would the communication.

I concluded that, to use a metaphor from carpentry, we need to measure twice but cut once. PR firms and communication departments were great at the cutting. And that had to be done precisely. But what was missing was a rigorous method of measurement – a way to prepare before cutting. And even to figure out whether to cut at all.

After 22 years doing crisis work for other firms and companies, I started Logos Consulting Group in 2002 as a focused crisis management, crisis communication, and executive leadership firm. We're not a PR firm. We don't reach out to media or investors, we don't do social media on behalf of clients; we don't send press releases. We don't do much communication implementation at all.

Rather, we help our clients think clearly, plan carefully, and execute effectively. We often work with their PR firms and with their in-house and external communication teams to build their ability to handle crises well. We even advise leading PR firms going through their own crises. But in all of it we keep our focus on the big picture. We operate at altitude. And we are more often brought in by the CEO, the board, the CFO, the general counsel, or other non-communicators.

And all our work, whether consulting, coaching, or executive education, begins with helping clients think clearly. Clear thinking is not easy, but it is the key to getting through crises well. And the decisions clients need to make in the moment of crisis can be agonizing. But they need to be made.

Far too often companies and leaders try to lessen the agony of decision by denial, deflection, or other things that make themselves feel good. But as a wise man once said, the only meaningful way to escape the agony of decision is by thinking.

We created the Logos Institute for Crisis Management and Executive Leadership in 2004 as a think tank and idea lab that would help our consulting practice apply best practices to client crises. And to provide tools, techniques, and materials to help clients think clearly and execute effectively.

This book is for leaders of organizations who need to be good stewards of reputation, trust, and competitive advantage; and for those who advise those leaders, whether in public relations, law, or other business disciplines.

This book is the first volume in the **Logos Institute Best Practices Series**, which will provide analysis and insight on a range of topics related to reputation, crisis, high-stakes communication, and similar areas. This first volume is on mental readiness as the key to managing crises effectively.

This is also the first volume more generally in our publishing imprint, **Logos Institute for Crisis Management and Executive Leadership Press**, which will more broadly produce written materials to help clients and students build their own capacity for leadership and effective communication, in crises and other high-stakes situations.

What all these books will have in common is this: they will stand at the intersection of scholarship and practice, providing both rigorous analysis and practical application of key principles. We hope you find this book, and the volumes yet to come, helpful.

Chapter 1:

Introduction: Mental Readiness

Why do some companies – and some governments, NGOs, and leaders – get through potentially catastrophic crises strong and successful, without any meaningful harm to reputation, to trust, to confidence, or to other measures of competitive advantage? And why do other companies – and governments, NGOs, and leaders – go through equivalent crises but come out the other side with their reputation in tatters, with trust and confidence evaporated, and with other measures of competitive advantage, from stock price to employee productivity, plummeting?

This book is about how leaders and the organizations they lead can maintain reputation, trust, confidence, financial and operational strength, and competitive advantage in a crisis. First, by thinking clearly; second by making smart choices; and third by executing those choices well.

I believe the difference between leaders who handle crises well and those who handle crises poorly is mental readiness: the ability some leaders exhibit that allows them to make smart choices quickly in a crisis. And this ability creates real competitive advantage.

One of the predictable patterns of crisis response is that the severity of the crisis event does not determine whether an organization and its leader get through a crisis well.

Indeed, two organizations, similarly situated, can see dramatically different outcomes based on the quality and timeliness of their individual responses to the crisis events. And the ability to respond effectively in a timely way is a consequence of mental readiness.

The former *Wall Street Journal* reputation beat reporter Ron Alsop, in his book *The 18 Immutable Laws of Corporate Reputation*, describes this pattern:

> Crises are inevitable – reputation damage isn't. Crises are a fact of life for both individuals and corporations. You can – and should – try to prevent them by managing your business and reputation well. But no matter how vigilant you are, crises arrive as certainly as death and taxes. How an individual or company reacts can be far more important than the circumstances of the crisis. It's the response that makes all the difference in minimizing damage to corporate reputation – and possibly even enhancing the image."[1]

It's the response that determines the outcome. In other words, it's what you do next that matters. And getting that right is not easy. It requires mental readiness.

Mental readiness involves habits of the mind: the persistent ability to remain calm, to think clearly, and to understand other people's concerns even as conditions deteriorate and as panic begins to strike all around the leader. But mental readiness requires preparation, as well as clear thinking, and both self-awareness and situational awareness.

The best leaders understand this.

Take, for example, American Express CEO Kenneth Chenault. He was quoted on the cover of a *Fortune* magazine special issue on effective leadership saying,

We have to remember that reputations are won or lost in a crisis.[2]

Inside the magazine, he elaborated:

One thing you learn is to understand thoroughly the attributes that are really important and focus on them so you're not just doing them unconsciously - you're conscious about it. It gives you an advantage. I say this all the time: Everyone can make a conscious choice to be a leader.[3]

Both statements are about mental readiness. The first, "We have to remember..." is specifically about a mental process. And the reason he admonishes leaders to remember that reputations can be both won and lost in a crisis – in the moment of crisis, when all eyes are on the leader, and at the very moment when the outcome is determined – is that leaders tend to forget. And then to act in counterproductive ways.

The second statement is about conscious deliberation about what matters. Again, a mental process. He notes that engaging in a conscious process gives an advantage – I call it a competitive advantage – that helps both the leader and the organization get through the worst of times. He also notes that becoming a leader involves, among other things, a conscious choice.

And just as leaders need to remember that reputations can be both won or lost in a crisis, I believe they also need to remember something even more important: Whether they win or lose their reputation in the crisis is completely within their control.

One of the persistent patterns in crises is that organizations and their leaders have far greater control over the outcome than they may originally imagine. To be sure, when something very bad has happened, they are unlikely to be able to undo damage. But they can prevent further damage, and can respond to the damage in ways that maintain or inspire trust and confidence. But for that they need to be prepared.

Three Dimensions of Mental Readiness

Mental Readiness

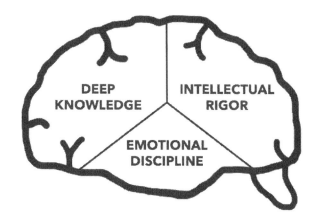

[Illustration by Holly Helstrom]

We can understand mental readiness as consisting of three separate but related dimensions: Emotional Discipline, Deep Knowledge, and Intellectual Rigor.

Emotional Discipline

Retired General Electric CEO Jack Welch, in the aftermath of the U.S. government's missteps after Hurricane Katrina, reflected on a common pattern of ineffective crisis management. In a *Wall Street*

Journal opinion piece, he described predictable stages of crises that are handled poorly:

> The first stage of that pattern is denial... The second is containment. This is the stage where people, including perfectly capable leaders, try to make the problem disappear by giving it to someone else to solve. The third stage is shame-mongering, in which all parties with a stake in the problem enter into a frantic dance of self-defense, assigning blame and claiming credit. Fourth comes blood on the floor. In just about every crisis, a high profile person pays with his job, and sometimes he takes a crowd with him.[4]

Welch says that one of the hallmarks of good leadership is to acknowledge the reality of what is happening without denial. He says leaders need to "dispense with denial quickly and look into the hard stuff with eyes open." And he describes the temperament that is best suited to handle crises: "a forthright, calm, fierce boldness."[5]

It's worth examining each of these attributes individually.

Forthright: A clear, unvarnished assessment of what is happening, what it likely means, and what the options are. Or, as Winston Churchill advised, "You must look at the facts because the facts look at you."

The first step to solving a problem is acknowledging that the problem exists. And then resolving the problem with what *Fortune* magazine, reflecting on American Express CEO Kenneth Chenault's leadership style, calls "industrial strength candor."[6]

Calm: Panic inhibits clear thinking. When under threat, the amygdala deep in the human brain shuts down the work of the pre-frontal cortex, the thinking part of the brain. This is known as an Amygdala Hijack, where emotions overtake clear thinking. That's why doctors advise their patients not to make any important life decisions in the immediate aftermath of a significant trauma, physical or emotional.

Effective leaders are able to remain calm even in the most dire of circumstances. Consider US Airways Captain Chesley Sullenberger, the pilot who performed the "Miracle on the Hudson" water landing. When CBS News's Katie Couric remarked at how calm he remained throughout the potentially catastrophic flight, he confessed that it was a forced calm. He said,

> The physiological reaction I had to this was strong, and I had to force myself to use my training and force calm on the situation.[7]

Even a forced calm works. And leaders and those whom they lead can be habituated to staying calm, even if it is a forced calm. For example, firefighters are trained to remain calm as they walk into a burning building. And soldiers are trained to move in the direction of gunfire, not to run away from it. In both cases their training, with repetition over time, creates new habits, including reprogramming the amygdala to not shut down thinking in times of stress.

One of the services Logos Institute for Crisis Management and Executive Leadership provides is crisis simulations. We engage leadership teams in real-world crises with compressed timelines and exaggerated consequences, forcing leaders to make decisions under great stress. After one very stressful simulation, roleplaying a hostile takeover attempt, and using the company's own investment bankers and lawyers to play out the sequence of a complex and fast-paced scenario over most of a day, the CEO told me,

This was the single most difficult day I've had since becoming CEO. I never want to go through this kind of stress in real life. So we need to constantly practice for events like this.[8]

That client, like many others, continues to war-game crisis scenarios to help all on the leadership team remain calm and make smart choices under stress.

Fierce: Even while being clear-eyed and not panicking, effective leadership also requires the ability to act quickly and decisively. One of the effects of panic is paralysis. An effective leader in crisis needs not only to think clearly but also to act decisively. Hesitation when action is called for causes loss of trust and and other dire consequences.

Bold: And boldness means that sometimes the actions that are called for are unpleasant. Indeed, in a crisis most choices are unattractive, and there is a tendency to try to resist making choices with suboptimal outcomes. Boldness means seeing the universe of choices and being able to make the choice that is most productive, even if unpalatable.

Emotional discipline also requires humility – so that the leader can understand what matters to others.

The best leaders take responsibility in a crisis by using what *Good to Great* author Jim Collins describes as the paradoxical combination of humility and fierce resolve.[9] Note that this is consistent with Jack Welch's description of the leadership attributes that the best leaders exhibit in a crisis: a forthright, calm, fierce boldness.

Humility isn't a word we often see in business. Humility all too often is interpreted as weakness, especially in competitive cultures like Wall Street, politics, or the top of big organizations.

But a dollop of humility tempers other attributes, and makes a leader even stronger. Humility helps a leader to recognize that maybe – just maybe – he or she might be wrong; that there may be other valid perspectives; that he or she doesn't have to be the smartest person in every room, at every meeting.

Humility also helps leaders to connect with others up, down, and across the chain of command; to build organizations and cultures that are more likely to thrive; to understand the perspectives of other stakeholders. As we will see in Chapter 3, Decision Criterion #1: What to Do, this ability to understand the perspectives of stakeholders is critical to getting through a crisis effectively.

Emotional intelligence guru Daniel Goleman, in a *Harvard Business Review* article "What Makes a Good Leader?," identifies self-awareness as the first leadership skill: "People with a high degree of self-awareness know their weaknesses and aren't afraid to talk about them."[10] He notes, however, that many executives mistake such candor for "wimpiness."

Jim Collins, author of *Good to Great*, also acknowledges the danger of misinterpreting humility for weakness. Like Welch and Goleman he notes that the most effective leaders are a study in duality:

> ...modest and willful, shy and fearless. To grasp this concept, consider Abraham Lincoln, who never let his ego get in the way of his ambition to create an enduring great nation... Those who thought Lincoln's understated manner signalled weakness in the man found themselves terribly mistaken.[11]

Indeed, Pope Francis, in a TED Talk recorded in April, 2017, noted that humility is not weakness; rather, it is a kind of fortitude:

> Please, allow me to say it loud and clear: the more powerful you are, the more your actions will have an impact on people, the more responsible you are to act humbly. If you don't, your power will ruin you, and you will ruin the other.[12]

The Pope used a metaphor to illustrate the consequence of having an imbalance of humility and resolve:

> There is a saying in Argentina: "Power is like drinking gin on an empty stomach." You feel dizzy, you get drunk, you lose your balance, and you will end up hurting yourself and those around you, if you don't connect your power with humility. Through humility... power... becomes a service, a force for good.[13]

Finally, humility recognizes that there's a big difference between responsibility and blame; that taking responsibility regardless of where the blame may lay down the organization is a first step in getting people to focus on a solution rather than simply point fingers.

Deep Knowledge

Deep knowledge includes having a significant understanding of the patterns that drive effective and ineffective crisis response, and in particular the reasons certain things work and certain things don't work – and never will.

Winston Churchill famously observed that good judgment is often the result of experience, and experience is often the result of poor judgment. But what if we could learn good judgment without suffering the consequences of poor judgment first?

Deep knowledge allows leaders to learn tough lessons without living those lessons directly – by studying the missteps of other leaders, and therefore preventing themselves from making the same mistakes. (See Chapter 5 for examples of such missteps.)

And deep knowledge also allows leaders to learn from other leaders' smart decision-making. That way they can give themselves permission to make choices that might otherwise seem too risky.

The U.S. Secretary of Defense, retired Marine four-star general James Mattis, is famous among Marines for his advocacy of reading in general and of the Marine Corps Commandant's Professional Reading List in particular. In a blog interview for the King's College London Department of War Studies, he said that reading is one important way to enhance deep knowledge, and therefore mental readiness:

> By reading, you learn through others' experiences, generally a better way to do business, especially in our line of work where the consequences of incompetence are so final for young men.
>
> Thanks to my reading, I have never been caught flat-footed by any situation, never at a loss for how any problem has been addressed (successfully or unsuccessfully) before. It doesn't give me all the answers, but it lights what is often a dark path ahead. Ultimately, a real understanding of history means that we face nothing new under the sun."[14]

The body of knowledge most relevant to crisis management, elaborated more fully later in this book, includes not only what works and doesn't work, but WHY. And it is the WHY that matters most. Because the WHY allows a leader to recognize that however tempting a course of action may seem, if it clearly will not work (because it never works – or never works in these circumstances) then the leader shouldn't even try it.

Pixar, Deep Knowledge, and the Power of Crisis Prevention

One of the best examples of harvesting deep knowledge and pattern recognition is the story of Pixar Animation Studios as it faced two critical inflexion points: grappling with initial success, and then a merger with a corporate giant.

As recounted in his 2014 book, *Creativity, Inc.*, Pixar president and co-founder Ed Catmull was determined to avoid the mistakes he had seen other Silicon Valley companies make throughout the 1980s and 1990s as Catmul and his co-founders were building Pixar:

> The leaders of these companies seemed so focused on the competition that they never developed any deep introspection about other destructive forces that were at work.[15]

This inspired Catmull and the rest of Pixar's leaders to place extraordinary value on paying attention to their internal and external surroundings. What he called their deep introspection led to a collective dedication to developing both self-awareness and situational awareness, and attention to whether they might be falling into destructive patterns. They continually asked constructive questions of themselves and used those answers to make smart business decisions. Says Catmull,

> I asked myself: If Pixar is ever successful, will we do something stupid, too? Can paying careful attention to the mistakes of others help us be more alert to our own? Or is there something

about becoming a leader that makes you blind to the things that threaten the well-being of your enterprise?"[16]

One of the patterns Catmull and his team saw was the tendency of successful companies to become set in their ways, to become complacent, and to stop learning new things.

It wasn't enough to be merely aware of the pattern. Catmull believed that such learning needed to be part of the structure of the company, part of the every-day experience of working at Pixar.

After the company's first film, in 1995, Pixar launched Pixar University (PU), a professional development program for the studio's new hires that soon became mandatory for all employees, including senior leadership. Pixar University's curriculum ranges from practical to recreational, offering courses in computer programing and drawing, but also in more esoteric fields such as fencing and belly dancing. Says Catmull,

> The purpose of P.U. was to send a signal about how important it is for every one of us to keep learning new things. That, too, is a key part of remaining flexible: keeping our brains nimble by pushing ourselves to try things we haven't tried before. I believe it makes us stronger.[17]

Catmull credits Pixar University as demonstrating to all Pixar employees the importance of keeping their brains and emotions nimble by constantly learning new things, and testing the boundaries of their capabilities and comfort levels. And it also gave them the self-confidence to be bold, even under pressure.

> Creativity involves missteps and imperfections. I wanted our people to get comfortable with that idea – that both the

organization and its members should be willing, at times, to operate on the edge.[18]

Another pattern that Catmull and his team saw in other companies was a tendency for creative meetings to be hijacked by non-creative types – accountants, lawyers, and people from other functional areas. As a result, what should have been creative choices were often compromised by other factors.

To prevent similar missteps, Pixar created Braintrust, an internal peer review group, consisting strictly of creative people with filmmaking experience, to assess a film's progress and to offer constructive criticism as a film was being made. The Braintust had strict rules on who could give advice, and who the ultimate arbiter of decisions would be – the film's director. All notes were given as suggestions, not as prescriptions, and the director could take or leave any given suggestion. Catmul says,

> The Braintrust's notes are intended to bring the true causes of problems to the surface. We believe that ideas – and thus, films – only become great when they are challenged and tested... I like to think of the Braintrust as Pixar's version of peer review, a forum that ensures we raise our game – not by being prescriptive but by offering candor and deep analysis."[19]

Catmull says that Braintrust encouraged the type of strategic thinking and effective decision making that not only prevented the predictable missteps of other successful companies. It also provided a culture that has allowed the studio to thrive since 1986, produce 16 consecutive number one films and even to survive a merger with its much larger corporate competitor, the Walt Disney Company, with its own cultural integrity intact.

When the Walt Disney Company purchased Pixar Animation Studios for $7.4 billion in January 2006, the deal was initially met with apprehension from both parties. Just two years earlier, good will between the studios plummeted when Disney's CEO Michael Eisner and Pixar's CEO Steve Jobs had a nasty falling out over terms of their longstanding distribution partnership.

Bob Iger replaced Eisner as Disney CEO in 2005, and quickly reached out to Pixar's leadership to mend fences and propose joining forces. When Iger took the helm at Disney, the studio had not produced a hit animated film in 16 years. It was his belief that the leaders at Pixar, specifically Ed Catmull and Pixar creative director John Lasseter were the only people capable of restoring Disney's animation department to the success it once had with films like *The Lion King* and *Aladdin*.

After meeting with Iger, who voiced his respect for Pixar's leadership acumen and pledged his allegiance to protecting its unique culture, Jobs, Catmull and Lasseter agreed to the merger.

Catmul later recalled,

> John [Lasseter] and I suddenly had the rare opportunity to take the ideas we'd honed over decades at Pixar and test them in another context. Would our theories about the necessity of candor, fearlessness, and self-awareness bear out in this new environment?[20]

One of the patterns that Catmul and the senior leaders were keenly aware of was the tendency of large buyers to swallow their smaller acquisitions, and then to homogenize them into the dominant culture of the acquirer.

This would have been deadly to the future success of Pixar and its brand, and would also have made the Disney purchase a waste of money. But Disney wasn't just buying a studio; it was buying a state of mind. Says Catmull,

> Something unusual had been built at Pixar and [Iger] wanted to understand it. For the first time in all the years that Pixar and Disney had worked together, someone from Disney was asking what we were doing that made our company different."[21]

The task of merging these two companies successfully fell largely on the shoulders of Catmull and Lasseter, named the respective president and creative director for both studios.

Fortunately, Iger and Jobs offered them guidance from firsthand experience on what works in a merger and what to avoid. Based on their advice, Catmull and Lasseter realized that they needed to create both the perception and the reality that Disney employees were not getting a bailout from the more talented studio. They also needed Pixar employees to believe they were not getting steamrolled by their larger corporate competitor.

Their strategy then, was twofold: *earn* the trust and confidence of their new Disney employees, and *maintain* the trust and confidence of their Pixar employees. Catmull and Lasseter developed a three-pronged approach to execute these strategies:

First, both studios were kept entirely separate, physically and bureaucratically.

In addition to maintaining separate physical studios, under no circumstances could either studio borrow staff from the other, no matter how tight a deadline or understaffed a project may be.

One might expect such an approach to create unhealthy resentment or competition between the studios. But it had the effect of earning Disney's employees' trust and maintaining Pixar's.

Keeping the studios separate sent the message that the studios' leaders believed each was strong enough to stand on its own and to solve its own problems. As a result, each team could maintain a sense of ownership and pride over their work without it being diminished by a bailout from the other studio. Catmull explains,

> There was an overarching management principle [behind this decision] at work as well. Not allowing borrowing was a conscious choice on our part to force problems to the surface where we could face them head on.[22]

Second, the Braintrust model was brought to Disney. Before the merger Disney's film directors would receive three sets of critiques from Disney's upper management – people with no movie-making experience – and were required to incorporate each of their stipulations, even when different people's input was contradictory. The creative side of Disney's business was completely overridden by managerial processes, and its movies suffered because of it for 16 years.

Catmull explains,

> None of the people giving these notes had ever made a film before, and the notes often conflicted with one another, creating a sort of schizophrenic quality to the feedback. This concept…could only result in an inferior product."[23]

One of the first things Catmull and Lasseter did was introduce the Braintrust model to Disney's directors by having them observe one of Pixar's Braintrust meetings. It took a few years for its principles to come naturally, but introducing the Braintrust and this new way of thinking shifted the decision-making power back into the most knowledgeable hands at Disney, the creatives, and not the business managers.

Third, a major concern of Pixar employees before the merger was that the unique elements of their culture were in jeopardy of being swallowed up in Disney's bureaucracy. Not only did Catmull and Lasseter ensure this would not happen by keeping the studios separate, they took it one step further by drawing up a document outlining all the things that would remain the same within Pixar, post-merger. The document, *The Seven Year Compact Plan*, included practical items regarding HR policy and health benefits, as well as concerns unique to Pixar, such as the continuation of their annual paper airplane contest and Cinco de Mayo party.

Catmull explains the significance of the *Compact* as follows:

> We couldn't say for sure that these items were what had propelled us to such success, but we felt strongly about them. We were different, and since we believe being different helps us maintain our identity, we wanted them to remain that way.[24]

The *Compact* succeeded in reassuring Pixar's employees that they could continue to trust in their leaders to protect the things they cared about most.

It has been more than a decade since Catmul first wondered whether the principles he developed within Pixar would be sustainable in another environment. In that time the commercial and critical success of Disney and Pixar films released since the merger would indicate a resounding yes.

Disney Animation has released four number one animated films since then, breaking its 16-year dry spell; even four years after its release *Frozen* is still the highest grossing animated film ever made.

Catmull says that in observing the turnaround in Disney's animation department, what made him most proud was that it was populated almost entirely by the same people who had been there before the merger.

At the same time, Pixar has continued its anomalous streak of success; two of its films released post-merger, *Toy Story 3* and *Finding Dory*, generated more than $1 billion each in box office receipts worldwide. Both studios are regular contenders for, and winners of, the Oscar for Best Animated Feature.

In Pixar we see how harvesting the experiences of other companies without having to make the same mistakes helps a company make smart decisions that not only prevent crises from happening in the first place, but that also create a sound and compelling culture and business.

And the same discipline allowed the Pixar brand and culture to survive one of the biggest threats, being subsumed into a larger, more dominant culture.

This deep knowledge was a critical element of Pixar's success. So was emotional discipline, allowing the leaders and their teams to stay focused even in very stressful times.

And the insights one harvests from deep knowledge provide both the confidence for and context in which to understand the third element of mental readiness, Intellectual Rigor.

Intellectual Rigor

There is a rigor to effective crisis management that is equivalent to the rigor found in other business processes. But that rigor is often unknown, ignored, or misapplied by many leaders, to their own and their organizations' misfortune. Indeed, one of the common patterns in crises is that leaders who exhibit rigor in all other elements of their work throw rigor to the wind when a crisis hits. And then are surprised when things go badly.

Clear Thinking: Name the Problem

Rigor begins with clarity of thinking. The economist and Christian theologian Michael Novak, in *The Spirit of Democratic Capitalism*, said that "The first of all moral obligations is to think clearly."[25]

He meant this first as a way of organizing society. But it applies also to leadership in general. The leader is, among many other things, a steward of the organization he or she leads. The CEO has a moral duty to put the interests of that organization first, even if it means doing things that are unpleasant or even painful.

Part of intellectual rigor is naming the problem to be solved. As General Electric's former CEO Jack Welch noted, one of the persistent patterns in ineffective crisis response is denial. Sometimes the denial comes in the form of ignoring a problem. But sometimes it consists of only partially acknowledging the problem, or ignoring the severity of the problem. (See Chapter 5 for more detailed descriptions of these kinds of denial.)

But sometimes the denial is in the form of failing to recognize the full significance of the problem; of misnaming the problem. Intellectual rigor insists on accurately naming the problem. Otherwise it will be virtually impossible to develop a solution that actually resolves the problem.

General Motors Cobalt

One example: In early 2014 Mary Barra, a long-time General Motors executive, became the company's CEO. Barra inherited a long-simmering crisis. Surprisingly, she had been previously unaware of it. For more than 12 years General Motors had known about a defect involving a poorly-designed ignition switch built into its Cobalt and other car lines.

That switch had a tendency to fail while the vehicle was in motion, with the result that the car turned itself off, and with it the power systems and airbags. More than a dozen people had been killed because of the defect, but the company had yet to recall the cars.

In mid-2014 GM paid a $35 million fine and the company recalled more than 20 million vehicles.[26] The company's board hired a highly respected independent lawyer to conduct a thorough investigation of what happened and why. That report was published at the end of May, 2014. It was devastating. It concluded:

> The below-specification switch approved in 2002 made its way into a variety of vehicles, including the Chevrolet Cobalt. Yet GM did not issue a recall for the Cobalt and other cars until 2014, and even then the initial recall was incomplete. GM personnel's inability to address the ignition switch problem for 11 years is a history of failures.[27]

But what is most interesting is the reason the report gave. In a series of missteps, the company had failed to name the problem correctly.

The report concludes that the engineers who investigated the crashes didn't understand a critical feature of the cars in question: when the engine turned off, the airbags were also disconnected. So were the power steering and power breaks. The engineers did not understand the significance of the engine turning off. They called it a "moving stall," and assumed that it could be easily corrected while driving. As a result, they labeled the issue a "customer inconvenience" rather than a safety issue.

So when it came time to discuss solutions, the Cobalt ignition problem got little priority, as engineers focused first on safety concerns, and only eventually got around to inconvenience issues. The report notes:

> GM personnel viewed the switch problem as a 'customer convenience' issue - something annoying but not particularly problematic - as opposed to the safety defect it was.[28]

And when solutions were proposed, cost weighed heavily on their decisions, which would not have been the case for a safety issue.

> Once so defined, the switch problem received less attention, and efforts to fix it were impacted by cost considerations that would have been immaterial had the problem been properly categorized in the first instance. Indeed, in this same decade, GM issued hundreds of recalls at great expense (including at times when its financial condition was precarious) because in the great majority of instances, it correctly determined or agreed that the issues that came to its attention implicated safety and demanded prompt action. But in the case of the Cobalt, it did not do so.[29]

Since recognizing the scope of the problem General Motors has responded robustly. It has offered $600 million in compensation for victims and their families, including payment for 124 deaths. In 2015 the company entered into a deferred prosecution agreement with the U.S. Department of Justice, forfeiting $900 million. The U.S. Attorney for the Southern District of New York, announcing the settlement with GM, said,

> For nearly two years, GM failed to disclose a deadly safety defect to the public and its regulator. By doing so, GM put its customers and the driving public at serious risk. Justice requires the filing of criminal charges, detailed admissions, a significant financial penalty, and the appointment of a federal monitor. These measures are designed to make sure that this never happens again.[30]

In General Motors' case, the misnaming of the problem had profound consequences, including more than 100 deaths, and led to the company ignoring genuine safety concerns for more than a decade.

Mental readiness requires not only having clarity about the actual problem, but also challenging assumptions about problems when the explanations seem not to make sense.

Company A: The *60 Minutes* Problem

Several years ago one of our clients[31] – a financial services company we'll call Company A – mobilized significant public relations and legal resources because the television news program *60 Minutes* was planning a profile on one of the client's business practices. That's because lawyers suing the company on behalf of thousands of customers wanted to put pressure on the company. When I arrived on the scene I was struck by the way people within the company, from the senior-most management through the public relations department, described the problem: "We have a *60 Minutes* problem… How are we going to address the *60 Minutes* problem?"

The client's lawyers described the *60 Minutes* situation as just a continuation of litigation, and referred to it as a legal problem. And because the matter was in litigation, they counseled silence. The more I probed into the situation, the more I – and a small cadre of business and communication people in Company A – recognized that the company had misnamed the problem.

By labeling it a *60 Minutes* problem, Company A's energies were focused on responding to the news program, worrying about employee and customer response to the program, and ignoring the fact that the company had business practices that were severely lacking in controls and that had caused harm to its customers. But because the matter had been in litigation for years, the company had been conditioned by its lawyers to be silent about the problems with the business practices.

Here's why misnaming the problem is harmful: Even if Company A had been able to persuade *60 Minutes* not to pursue the story – a very unlikely event – the problem would not have gone away. Even though the "*60 Minutes* problem" would be solved, the same adversary lawyers who took the story to *60 Minutes* could as easily have interested *The New York Times*, *The Wall Street Journal*, or any other media. And the underlying business practices would continue to go unaddressed, potentially disadvantaging more customers and giving rise to more dissatisfied customers, litigation, and negative visibility.

And because the program would likely have aired regardless of the company's response, misnaming the problem would cause the company to allocate its resources to get its employees and customers not to take the program seriously.

But the problem wasn't that a prominent television news program was planning a negative story. The problem was that the company had ignored indefensible business practices. And now its adversaries were taking the opportunity to cast the company in the worst possible light.

It took considerable energy and persistence on the part of the small group of leaders within Company A's organization, but the company was persuaded to overhaul its business practices, establish and enforce new standards of conduct among those who implemented the business practices, and pay compensation to customers who had been negatively affected by it. The company announced these changes before the *60 Minutes* program aired, to no particular fanfare, and began to implement them. The goal of the announcement wasn't to promote the new business practices, but rather to show that the company had recognized a fundamental business problem, had taken decisive action, and had communicated it clearly. In other words, to show that the company was not indifferent to the harm suffered by its customers. (See Decision Criterion #1: What to Do, Chapter 3.)

The *60 Minutes* program came and went, and it was very negative, essentially tracking the narrative that was playing out in the class-action litigation, and mentioning the company's remedial action only in passing.

But in the immediate aftermath of the program, as other media and the company's regulators began to explore the problem, it became clear to them that the company had already owned up to its responsibilities and that its customers were no longer at risk. No other media did stories on the business practices in question. And the company's regulators, who initiated an investigation following the *60 Minutes* story, eventually commended Company A for having already taken the action the regulators would have required.

Moreover, the offending business practices were discontinued, thereby reducing the future likelihood of dissatisfied customers, potential litigation, and negative visibility.

So naming the problem, in plain English and without euphemism, is an essential part of intellectual rigor, of thinking clearly.

Misnaming the problem is counterproductive for two reasons. First, it leaves the fundamental problem unaddressed, dealing only with the symptoms of the problem rather than solving the problem itself. And second, it gives management false hope: the illusion that it is managing the crisis, when in fact it's compounding the difficulties. So when the crisis becomes public, the company's first response will predictably be inadequate, and the result will be both loss of stakeholder trust and surprise on management's part that what it had planned didn't work.

And in the case of a regulated company, regulators would learn not only about the problem but also about the fact that the company had been indifferent to the problem. The company would then need to be in full damage-control mode, which could easily have been avoided by a more deliberate diagnosis of the problem.

Company B: The *Fortune* Magazine Problem

One other example: I was called into a crisis by a public relations firm and its client, a well-known corporation that we'll call Company B. The PR firm and head of corporate communication for Company B briefed me on what they called "a *Fortune* magazine" problem.

They said that *Fortune* magazine was working on a story about Company B's chairman, a charismatic person who had been very successful but who also had some personal issues: he had borrowed many millions of dollars from the company and banks to support a lavish lifestyle – a private jet, a number of palatial homes around the world. But he was now in personal financial distress. Some large investors and investment analysts were asking questions about his accountability during his tenure as CEO before becoming chairman. He was also well connected politically, and contributed heavily to one of the nation's most visible but divisive politicians. He also had personal enemies who were not averse to calling attention to his distress. Company B was also concerned about the weakness in the price of its stock, and fearful that continued stock decline could make it subject to a hostile takeover. Indeed, takeover rumors were already circulating on Wall Street.

The more I listened, the more I concluded that the problem had been misnamed. Company B did not have a *Fortune* magazine problem. It had a problem with its chairman. Even if *Fortune* could be persuaded not to write its story, the company would still be at risk.

The chairman's adversaries – both business and political – could continue to feed the media negative information until someone published it, at which time investors would clearly be concerned. And with the threat of a takeover looming, any stock weakness would trigger events that could result in the company losing control of its destiny.

I met with Company B's CEO, CFO, general counsel, and some members of the board of directors. They were initially shocked by the realization that their problem was bigger than just an inconvenient media inquiry. But they came to the meeting with open eyes and open minds. We worked through a number of scenarios that all reached the same conclusion: the chairman had to go. Under any of the scenarios we worked through, the chairman's continued affiliation with the company led to very negative outcomes. Under the same scenarios his quiet and dignified departure led to positive outcomes.

Company B's board of directors met without its chairman and reviewed the situation and the various scenarios. They saw the wisdom of asking the chairman to retire and requiring that he immediately repay the loans from the company – even if that meant he had to sell his houses or plane. They recognized that if *Fortune* ran its story, Company B would be better served by having the focus be a former chairman who had repaid loans, rather than the current chairman who owed the company millions.

Within two weeks the chairman announced his retirement and repaid his outstanding loans to the company, on time and with interest. The stock price climbed, and there was no hostile takeover. *Fortune* never ran its story.

Clear Thinking: Take the Pain

Intellectual rigor isn't just about naming the problem. It's also about understanding consequences.

In particular, intellectual rigor is about understanding one of the patterns we see across all forms of crisis: The longer it takes to do what is necessary, the harder it will be to maintain the trust and confidence of those who matter.

One way to think about it is that taking the pain in the short term results in far less pain than delaying, which only makes matters much worse. (See Chapter 4, Decision Criterion #2: When).

One of the principles of effective crisis response is this: Do what you know you will have to do anyway, but when it can do you some good.

For example, if it is clear that the only way to maintain trust is to apologize, then apologize early. If you wait until there are extensive public calls for an apology, the apology itself will seem coerced, or insincere, or insufficient. But an early apology shuts down that very negative dynamic. Similarly, if someone needs to be fired, fire that person quickly.

Over the past 20 years, I have had discussions with boards of directors or executive committees of dozens of clients, focused on the predictable consequences of pending negative events. These ranged from the discovery of malfeasance, improper accounting of off-balance sheet financings, excessive borrowing by CEOs from the company, in one case without the knowledge of the board of directors, and even fraud.

In each case the discussion led to the conclusion that the chairman, CEO, or other senior executive might need to be replaced.

The starting point of these discussions was usually something far more benign: What can we expect if the worst happens (if the SEC throws the book at us; if we're indicted; if we lose this lawsuit, etc.)?

Most clients took the situation seriously, disclosed fully, and took decisive action – in one case replacing the CEO that week, even before the anticipated event had happened. In other cases the clients immediately resolved and disclosed the accounting issues, restated earnings for the prior two years, announced new accounting procedures, and established stronger controls to prevent similar problems from recurring. In all cases the clients' stock remained at pre-crisis levels, and the clients, despite suffering a great emotional toll, found that the crises caused no lasting reputational or operational harm. It's not that they didn't have a crisis, or that the crisis was averted. Rather, the crisis – the turning point – was managed in such a way that reputational, financial, and operational harm was avoided.

But a few clients didn't have either the emotional discipline or the intellectual rigor to make smart choices that quickly. They delayed, denied, resorted to incomplete solutions, prevaricated, or otherwise failed to be effective leaders. And in all those cases the consequences were severe, including stock price collapses, significant fines and penalties, and eventual CEO firings. But only after much damage had been done.

Company C: Taking the Pain

In one typical case, – we'll call it Company C – I worked the board of directors through an exercise in anticipation of a very significant corporate setback that was possible in the near future. A highly-contested legal proceeding could go one of two ways. If in a negative direction, there could be serious long-term harm to the strategic position and operations of Company C. The company was confident that it could handle a positive outcome. But it hadn't thought through how to handle a negative decision.

We began by assuming a negative decision, and reviewed how each stakeholder group would predictably think and feel, and what it would predictably do upon hearing the news. And also what each stakeholder group would say to others, to its own members, and to management.

We reviewed what the news media and social media would do on Day 1, what customers would do, what competitors would do, what investors would do, and what regulators would do, and how each would respond to what the others did and said. And we projected consequences, on employee morale and loyalty, on stock price, etc. We then played this out day-by-day for the first week, and then week-by-week for a month. The board concluded that the inevitable consequence of that course of events was that the CEO would need to resign sometime in the third or fourth week. But by then the company would have been subjected to several weeks of very bad news, of employee morale plummeting, of customer defections, of predatory behavior by competitors, of severe regulatory scrutiny, of stock price drops, and of distractions preventing management from running the company effectively.

We then played out the same scenario with the assumption that the CEO would resign immediately when the negative decision took place. What would each stakeholder group think and feel upon hearing the news both of the setback and of the CEO's resignation? What would the media say on Day 1? What would customers, investors, employees, regulators, and competitors do? And what would be the consequences on employee morale and loyalty, on stock price, etc.? We played the scenario out day-by-day for the first week, and week-by-week for four weeks. The board, including the CEO, quickly concluded that under this scenario the CEO's reputation would suffer less, the company's reputation, operations, and stock price would suffer less, management would be able to get back to work sooner, and the company would be far better off.

Company C's board then assigned a small working group to validate all the assumptions of the scenarios, to work through two parallel paths of action and communication, and to assure that the scenario as discussed would genuinely play out. The working group concluded that it would.

The working group then projected all the possible ways the negative event could occur, and defined a worst case in which the CEO's resignation was inevitable, and a less-bad case in which the legal outcome wouldn't be quite as severe, and in which the CEO's departure would not be inevitable, at least not right away.

The working group then did one last piece of due diligence: It developed parallel communication plans: one for a negative decision below the threshold requiring the CEO to leave immediately – essentially a wait-and-see – and a second plan for a worst case.

On the day the event occurred, the news was very bad. It was the worst case that Company C had feared. The CEO resigned immediately, and the communication plan drafted with the resignation in mind was implemented. The new CEO, who had been pre-selected by the board, was formally named. When employees arrived at work there were voicemails and emails from the departing CEO and also from the new CEO. The new CEO had a conference call with the senior leadership team worldwide, confirming the company's business strategy and outlining the communication plan for the coming days and weeks, including having meetings with their employees that day. The new CEO did an early wire service interview, which was picked up by all the morning business television programs. When the market opened at 9:30 am, the complete package of news was available to the investment marketplace: the corporate setback, the CEO's resignation, the new CEO's appointment, and confirmation of the company's business strategy into the future. The new CEO then spoke with investors on a conference call.

There was one day of negative news; there were three days of future-looking stories about the company under new leadership. The stock dipped a bit but recovered. There was no meaningful drop in employee morale, no predatory behavior by competitors, no severe regulatory scrutiny, nor any of the other events that were predicted to take place if the CEO had remained.

Company C did itself, its shareholders, and its employees a great service by thinking clearly about the consequences of the pending negative event, and by recognizing that time was its enemy. It took the pain early to avoid much worse pain later.

It took decisive action in the turning-point moment, when it had the optimal opportunity to control the outcome. And it demonstrated how effective crisis management is a competitive advantage: the company remained strong despite the setback, demonstrably stronger than it would have been if it hadn't thought through the predictable consequence – both intended and unintended – of a negative decision.

Very often taking the pain requires taking actions that in the short term may cause inconvenience, embarrassment, discomfort, financial cost, or other distress. But done right, short-term pain now can prevent much greater pain later.

There is a greater than incremental advantage in doing what is necessary to fix a problem as early in the crisis as possible, even at the cost of embarrassment, discomfort, financial loss, or even physical pain. In most cases, companies eventually get around to fixing the problem, but they do so only after suffering significant reputational, operational, or financial harm. This is often avoidable, as we saw in the example of Company C, which concluded that both the company and its CEO would be best served if the CEO resigned immediately upon a worst-case negative event.

In the case of that company, it was certainly painful for the board to conclude that the CEO, who had done a very good job, would be expected to step down as a tangible gesture of accountability for the company's setback. It was certainly painful for the CEO to recognize that his career was at an end: that he probably wouldn't be CEO of a major company again.

But in the agony of their deliberations, the board's clear thinking allowed the leaders to have confidence in the most productive course of action. Both the CEO and the board recognized that the CEO's departure was inevitable; that the only issue was when, and that an earlier departure would result in less pain to him and to the company in the long term, however painful it was in the short term.

Similarly, Company A, the subject of the *60 Minutes* broadcast, could have avoided pain in the short term by continuing to behave as if the problem was the *60 Minutes* program itself rather than an indefensible business practice. But it took the pain in the short term, including the painful admission that it had allowed the situation to go unaddressed for years because of litigation fears. It too agonized over its decision. But clear thinking gave its leaders confidence about successful resolution of the crisis. And in the long-term the company suffered far less pain and disruption.

Equally important, it directed its resources toward actually solving the underlying business problem, not merely addressing the symptom of the problem, the *60 Minutes* broadcast. This made for a more efficient use of the company's resources, and put the company in the strong position to have confidence that its actions would actually protect its competitive position, rather than give false comfort.

And finally, Company B, which had the governance problem, took the pain in recognizing that the only viable solution to its problem was for the chairman to retire.

The chairman also took the pain, in a number of ways. First, he stopped being the chairman of a prominent publicly-traded company. Second, he found ways to repay the significant loans the company had made to him, and he did so at considerable personal cost. But he also knew that the alternatives were worse. First, he would have to leave the company anyway, possibly in ways that were less attractive than retiring. Second, he would need to repay the money anyway. And finally, his personal reputation would have been tarnished either way. Far better for him as well as for Company B for him to retire quietly.

And while it may be understandable that people, even those with a fiduciary duty to shareholders, may wish to avoid embarrassment, unpleasantness, and pain, it is also notable that having the character to own up to one's mistakes can not only prevent greater pain in the future, it can even enhance a company's stature.

The classic example of this is Johnson & Johnson, which took great pain when it recalled its Tylenol® products in the wake of a poisoning scandal in 1982. The company spent millions in the recall and lost sales. But because of the actions it took, it was seen to care about the harm suffered by those who took Tylenol® tablets that had been tampered with. For decades after the Tylenol® crisis, Johnson & Johnson was consistently ranked as one of the most respected companies in the United States.

Shareholders typically reward companies that take crises seriously. *The Wall Street Journal* profiled a study by two University of Michigan professors and a Stanford Graduate School of Business professor which showed that companies that took responsibility for their crises outperformed the shares of companies that passed the buck.

> Of course it is human nature for individuals to blame others or external factors when things go wrong because doing so helps preserve their self-esteem while boosting their image to others. But shareholders apparently like companies that own up to their mistakes because doing so implicitly sends a message that they are in control over their business and have the ability to make the changes that will turn performance around. 'Shareholders prefer companies that take the heat, rather than companies that just make excuses,'[one of the study's authors, Michigan professor Fiona] Lee said.[32]

Professor Lee's study found that companies that took responsibility for their crises outperformed those that blamed other factors by between 14 percent and 19 percent. An earlier study by Professor Lee found that subordinates were more likely to be favorably disposed toward bosses who took responsibility for negative events, including salary cuts and pay freezes.

Key Takeaways from This Chapter

One of the predictable patterns of crisis response is that the severity of the crisis event does not determine whether an organization gets through the crisis successfully. Rather, the timeliness and effectiveness of the response does.

But timeliness and effectiveness are byproducts of mental readiness, which we define as a combination of emotional discipline, deep knowledge, and intellectual rigor.

Emotional Discipline: Every crisis takes place in an environment of emotional resonance: of fear, anger, anguish, embarrassment, shame, or panic. Effective leaders are able to control negative emotions and to remain calm. Even a forced calm can help a leader make smart choices by continuing to think clearly despite having a strong emotional stimulus. As Captain Sullenberger noted, when his plane lost power he had a strong physiological reaction and had to draw on all his training to force calm on the situation. Emotional discipline also allows the leader to see the crisis for what it is, and to avoid the denial that is often a consequence of emotional response to a crisis.

Emotional discipline can be developed through training, through repetition, and through simulations. At Logos Institute we often run leadership teams through high-stress situations to build their ability to keep calm and think clearly.

Deep Knowledge: Deep knowledge starts with understanding the patterns that drive effective and ineffective crisis response, including the reasons certain things work and certain things don't work.

Deep knowledge includes not only what works and what doesn't work, but WHY. And it is the WHY that matters most. The WHY allows a leader to recognize that however a course of action may seem, if it clearly will not work, because it never works, then the leader should not even try.

With that insight leaders can then focus instead on what is likely to work.

Deep knowledge also includes studying particular crises, both effective and ineffective. This allows leaders to learn tough lessons without experiencing the trauma that took place among those who lived the crisis. That way they can give themselves permission to make choices that might otherwise seem risky.

We saw this in the management philosophy that led Pixar to avoid the mistakes of other Silicon Valley companies after initial success, and also to navigate their being bought by a much larger company while maintaining and enhancing their own value and their parent company's value.

Intellectual Rigor: There is rigor to effective crisis management that is equivalent to the rigor found in other business processes. But that rigor is often ignored or misapplied.

The rigor begins with clear thinking. The leader is, among other things, a steward of the organization he or she leads. The CEO has a moral duty to think clearly and to put the interests of the organization first, even if it means doing things that are unpleasant or even painful.

Part of intellectual rigor is naming the problem to be solved. Many leaders deny or ignore a problem, or understate the severity of the problem. But if a problem isn't named clearly it will be very difficult to solve the actual problem. Instead resources are spent trying to solve the symptoms of the problem.

Misnaming the problem is counterproductive for two reasons: First, it leaves the fundamental problem unaddressed. Second, it gives management false hope: the illusion that it is managing the crisis, when in fact it is compounding the difficulties.

Intellectual rigor is also about understanding consequences. That means taking the pain: doing what leaders already know they will need to do eventually, but doing it when it can have a positive effect. If it is clear that the only way to maintain trust is to apologize, then apologize quickly and fully. If it is clear that the CEO will need to be fired, fire him or her quickly. A late apology or late dismissal, after public outcry, will seem forced and insincere, and will come only after the loss of trust and other measures of competitive advantage.

While it is understandable that people, even those with a fiduciary duty to shareholders, may wish to avoid embarrassment, unpleasantness, and pain, it is also notable that having the character to own up to one's mistakes can not only prevent greater pain in the future; it can even enhance a company's stature.

Chapter 2:

Crisis Means Choice

Many leaders consider a crisis to be a moment when something bad has happened. I believe that this view is both incorrect and counterproductive.

As we saw in some of the examples at the end of Chapter 1, the moment of crisis often arises long before something bad has actually happened. By the time the event becomes public a predictable negative dynamic has already begun. Leaders need a more expansive understanding of the meaning of crisis if they are to manage crises well, and to do so at the time when a leader has maximum control over the outcome.

For example, the leaders of Pixar recognized that Silicon Valley companies historically had a problem dealing with their initial success. Instead of continuing to build on their core values, they would become excessively focused on competitors, and on protecting their market presence rather than growing it. And with success came a tendency to avoid learning or doing new things. Pixar knew it shouldn't wait for those problems to become a reality; it needed to prevent them. It needed to act at the right moment, before there had been harm. Pixar was in a crisis, even before the negative events had taken place.

The English word *crisis* derives from the ancient Greek word *krisis* (κρισισ),[33] which means decision, or choice, especially at a turning point where one's destiny is determined one way or another.

In the plot of every Greek tragedy there is a moment of *krisis* where the protagonist has to choose – for example, whether to murder his father and marry his mother.

We remember those choices more than two thousand years later only when the protagonists chose poorly: Oedipus chose poorly, and we now not only remember his poor choice, but give his name to a psychological syndrome of inappropriate attachment to one's mother.

But we don't remember those who chose wisely – indeed, those choices never became the subject of tragedies – the social media of their time.

The same applies with modern crises. We tend to remember those crises where leaders made poor choices – for example, General Motors' decade-plus-long delay in recalling Cobalt cars – but only rarely when leaders made wise choices. Test: Can you remember a well-handled automotive recall? There have been hundreds. When clients or students ask me, *What's the best-handled crisis you've experienced?* my response is to smile and say, *It's the one you never heard of.*

We continue to have vestiges of the idea of crisis as choice in English. Indeed, *criterion* – the basis of choice – is from a related Greek word *kriterion* (κριτηριον). *Critic* – the person who chooses what is good or bad – is from *krites* (κριτησ), or the one who can discern between good and bad.

Fink on Turning Points

The classic book on decision-making in crisis is Steven Fink's 1986 *Crisis Management: Planning for the Inevitable.*

Like the Greek understanding of *krisis*, Fink describes a crisis as a "turning point," not a necessarily negative event or bad thing. "It is merely characterized by a certain degree of risk and uncertainty."[34]

Fink refers to crises as "prodromal," or as precursors or predictors of something yet to come (Italics in original):

> From a practical, business-oriented point of view, a crisis (a turning point) is *any prodromal situation that runs the risk of:*
> A. Escalating in intensity.
> B. Falling under close media or government scrutiny.
> C. Interfering with the normal operations of business.
> D. Jeopardizing the positive public image presently enjoyed by a company or its officers.
> E. Damaging a company's bottom line in any way.[35]

Fink points out that as a turning point the crisis could go either way:

> If any or all of these developments occur, the turning point most likely will take a turn for the worse… Therefore, there is every reason to assume that if a situation runs the risk of escalating in intensity, that same situation – caught and dealt with in time – may not escalate. Instead, it may very conveniently dissipate, be resolved.[36]

Fink's approach to crises anticipates both catastrophic events and routine dealings that are suddenly the subject of attention. It finds merit in early intervention and affirmative management of business processes as well as the communications about the event.

In the Fink formulation, the prodromal event is the moment of choice.

Pixar understood that, and capitalized on that moment of choice, both in its early success and when it faced the prospect of being acquired by Disney.

Managing Choices

I believe that understanding crisis in the Greek sense – a moment of decision or choice, the turning point where one's destiny is determined either positively or negatively – is the key to effective crisis management.

And as with any other form of management, there is a rigor to getting it right.

But so many leaders who otherwise are gifted managers – managing finance, or engineering, or marketing, or any other professional discipline, or even a whole company – throw rigor to the wind when a crisis emerges. Then they either make up a response on the fly or try to cobble together bits of knowledge from other parts of their experience. Or they ignore the crisis until it is too late.

And the starting point of that rigor is to have clarity about the crisis in the first place. In Chapter 1 we explored the consequences of not naming the problem accurately. The rigor in naming the problem begins with a series of questions intended to help us understand what is happening, how it is likely to unfold, what it means, who might be affected, and so on.

And once we have clarity about the problem, the rigor also includes identifying a set of options of how we might respond, and projecting the outcomes for each option.

Then the discipline consists of making choices based not on personal preference, or fear, or denial, but rather based on the best set of outcomes – or, more precisely, the less bad set of outcomes.

The Less Bad Choice

We can see the power of the less bad choice in a scene from the classic film *Butch Cassidy and the Sundance Kid.*

In that 1969 western, Butch and Sundance, played respectively by Paul Newman and Robert Redford, are professional bandits in the late 1800s being pursued by a determined lawman and his posse. They ride their horses up a steep bluff, dismount, and slide down the other side of the hill, coming to rest on a narrow ledge on a gorge overlooking a roaring river some 150 feet below. The lawmen are taking positions on the hill above them. They are trapped.

They consider their options:

Butch: The way I figure it is we can either fight or give. If we give we go to jail... But if we fight, they can stay right where they are and starve us out. Or go for position, shoot us. Might even get a rock slide started, get us that way...[37]

They crouch with their backs to the hill as Sundance reloads his revolver. Then Butch realizes they have a third choice:

Butch: No, we'll jump.
Sundance: Like hell we will.
Butch: No, it will be OK, if the water's deep enough and we don't get squished to death. They'll never follow us.
Sundance: How can you know?
Butch: Would you make a jump like that [if] you didn't have to?
Sundance: I have to and I'm not gonna.

Butch: Well we got to, otherwise we're dead. They're just gonna have to go back down the same way they come. Come on. We got to!

Sundance: Get away from me.

Butch: Why?

Sundance: I want to fight them.

Butch: They'll kill us.

Sundance: Maybe.

Butch: Do you want to die?

Sundance: Do you?...

Butch: What's the matter with you?

Sundance: I can't swim!

Butch: (laughing hysterically) Why, you crazy? The fall will probably kill you![38]

They look at each other, and then simultaneously run and leap off the ledge. They land in the river, ride it down, and eventually escape.

In the agony of their decision, they knew that a jump that neither wanted to take was the only way to preserve the possibility of survival. In the event, it worked, and they were able to resume their bank robbing career outside the United States.

Their jump was not a leap of faith, but rather a recognition that a bad outcome was likely. But it was a less bad outcome than either surrendering or fighting against the odds.

Understanding the Problem

Making good choices starts with clarity about the problem itself. Understanding the problem requires rigor in asking questions in a certain order, and then discipline in answering those questions to achieve clarity about the situation and the likely consequence. Here's a productive sequence of questions that help foster situational awareness.

Question 1: What Do We Have?

The assessment of the crisis begins with a candid description of what happened, what is happening, or what might happen. Here there is a need for real discipline to avoid confusing or conflating the symptom with the cause. As in the example from Chapter 1, the presenting problem for Company A – *60 Minutes* called – is not the actual problem. That Company A has a business practice that has been harming customers, about which *60 Minutes* is now aware, is the actual problem.

This tendency to confuse the symptom with the cause is common because the people who receive the media inquiry (the media relations people in the public relations department) are typically not in a position to prescribe corporate policy, merely to speak with reporters. So the initial description of the risk the organization faces is often framed in terms of public visibility and communication, rather than in business terms. And we saw in the General Motors Cobalt case what happens when the problem is initially mis-identified.

Rigor also requires using candor to describe the problem as those who matter to the company are likely to describe it. This means avoiding indirect language or euphemism. Calling the crisis "a *60 Minutes* problem" isn't helpful.

Question 2: What Does It Mean?

Once we have named the problem, we then need to identify the significance of it. If left unattended, how will this play out? What are the likely consequences? It's important here to challenge assumptions. For example, in the General Motors Cobalt crisis GM engineers simply assumed that a car turning itself off while in motion could be turned back on without incident. That's a pretty big assumption, and one that is testable. If they had been able to see that a car turning itself off would also simultaneously cause the power brakes and power steering and the airbags to disengage, they could have seen that the likely consequences were dire, and that in fact the ignition problem was a significant safety issue.

Similarly, in the example of Company C that faced a difficult legal decision, one key to its making smart choices was playing out the predictable reactions of each stakeholder group, over time, thereby getting clarity about the likely consequences of delaying a decision on the CEO resigning.

Question 3: What Do We Want?

Getting clarity about what the problem is and what it means helps identify the goal: What is the ideal outcome we seek? Here we need to resist the temptation to wish that the crisis never happened. We can't un-ring a bell. But we can project a less bad outcome. More about outcomes just below.

Question 4: How Can We Make That Happen?

Once we have clarity about the desired outcome, we can begin to project how we can make that outcome happen. So consider Company A, with the so-called *60 minutes problem,* described above.

We could answer *Question 1, What Do We Have,* this way: We have a number of business practices that for years have disadvantaged customers. These business practices are coming under scrutiny in a lawsuit. *60 Minutes* is working on a story about the business practices. It is clear that the plaintiffs' lawyers got *60 Minutes* interested in the story. Even if *60 Minutes* were to not run it, the lawyers would find other national media who would be interested.

We could answer *Question 2, What Does It Mean,* this way: The business practice will soon be the subject of intense criticism, if not on *60 Minutes* then on other national media. That will generate the interest of regulators and concern among customers. It may also affect employee morale, and the company's overall reputation, and brand.

We could answer *Question 3, What Do We Want,* this way: We want to prevent adverse regulatory action and to protect our reputation and brand. We want to minimize the impact of a *60 Minutes* broadcast, and minimize the chances of other media piggy-backing off *60 Minutes.* The company could also add, We want to live our brand promise and treat all customers fairly; to the degree we are not doing so we need to fix this. (This proved to be a powerful argument that helped persuade the company's leadership to take responsible action.)

We can then answer *Question 4, How Can We Make That Happen,* this way: We can prevent most of the anticipated harm by recognizing that the business practices are inappropriate and unsustainable. We can discontinue the practices. We can identify the customers who were disadvantaged. And we can pay them compensation. We can announce the change in business practices before the *60 Minutes* broadcast airs. And we can be ready upon the broadcast to explain to employees and others what we have already done about the allegations made by *60 Minutes*.

In fact, this was precisely the analysis the client undertook. But making those choices, in the moment when the choices mattered, was very hard. It took a great deal of persuasion by a small group of company leaders to convince the senior-most levels of the company to take the pain.

The Power of Options and Outcomes

Managing choices includes recognizing that there is always more than one way to respond to any crisis.

That means that there are always options available. Sometimes the options present themselves clearly: We can do A, or B, or C. But sometimes it isn't clear what the options are. In those circumstances, it's useful to understand options in terms of magnitude:

➢   *Option 1: Do nothing* (or nothing out of the ordinary). In the case of Company C, with the pending negative legal decision, doing nothing would mean keeping the CEO in office.

➢   *Option 2: Do something small.* In the case of Company C, this would mean keeping the CEO in office and waiting to see whether it would be necessary to have him resign.

➤   *Option 3: Do something big.* In the case of Company C, this
     meant having the CEO resign immediately upon the negative
     decision.

But having the three options is not enough. It's critical to
project the likely outcomes of each option. And then to resist making
choices based on personal preference or denial. Rather, the choice
should be based on the outcomes that get us closer to our goal, in
Company C's case, minimal damage to stock price, employee morale,
and business competitiveness.

Thinking Clearly: Managing Our Choices

Crisis management is the management of choices – the
management of decisions that leaders make when things have the
potential to go very wrong.

Note that in a crisis most of the choices are unpleasant: even
the best choice is often still undesirable. So the best choice is usually
the less bad choice. The challenge is knowing which choice would be a
less bad choice, and then having the judgment (deep knowledge) and
the self-control (emotional discipline) to choose it despite its
unattractiveness.

Consider, again, Captain Chesley Sullenberger, who was
piloting US Airways flight 1549 on January 15th, 2009. About a minute
after taking off from LaGuardia Airport, and at 3,000 feet of altitude,
his plane flew through a flock of geese and became completely

disabled. He found himself in command of a 72-ton glider loaded with highly explosive jet fuel, and 155 people on board.

We can put ourselves in Captain Sullenberger's position and do a quick analysis, using the Understand the Problem questions we covered above, and then exploring options and outcomes:

Question 1: What Do We Have? Here the situation is quite clear. We have an aircraft at low altitude without any power, over a city, with fuel tanks filled with jet fuel, and with 155 people on board.

Question 2: What Does It Mean? The aircraft is essentially a glider. The controls unrelated to thrust continue to work, but there is no ability to accelerate or climb. So the plane will eventually come down, and soon. The fuel on the aircraft means that any landing on the ground risks a major explosion and fire, putting at risk not only the lives of the passengers and crew, but also of any people on the ground.

Question 3: What Do We Want? The goal is to prevent or minimize loss of life and injury, among the passengers and crew and among people on the ground.

Question 4: How Can We Make That Happen? We can minimize loss of life by directing the plane to a landing that is least likely to cause an explosion in a populated area.

But how to execute that strategy? Captain Sullenberger had a choice to make, among three options:

➤ *Option 1:* Return to LaGuardia. *Likely outcomes:* If he could not reach the airport, he would bring the plane down in a heavily populated urban area, with the possibility of massive loss of life on the ground. Even if he made it to LaGuardia he risked collisions with other aircraft on the ground, with potentially catastrophic consequences. If his angle onto the runway was not perfect, he risked veering off the runway and colliding into other planes. And without power he would be unable to use reverser thrusters, so he wouldn't be able to control the speed of the plane on the runway. LaGuardia runways are very short, and he might overshoot the runway, ending up in the East River. It quickly became clear to Captain Sullenberger that he was unlikely to return safely to the airport. And when directed to do so by the air traffic controller he responded that he was unable to do so.

➤ *Option 2:* Land at Teterboro airport in New Jersey. *Likely outcomes:* If he could not reach the airport the plane would come down in a heavily populated suburb, with the possibility of catastrophic loss of life. And as at LaGuardia, even if he made the runway, there was the risk of collisions with other aircraft.

➤ *Option 3:* Land in the Hudson River. *Likely outcomes:* The worst consequence would be that all 155 people on board, plus anyone on a ship with which the plane might collide in the river, would die. There was minimal risk of the fuel exploding and causing a massive fire; no population center at risk; no other planes, themselves laden with fuel, with which he might collide.

Captain Sullenberger concluded that the chances of getting back to LaGuardia or to Teterboro successfully were slim. So he chose to land in the Hudson River instead. No pilot wants to land in a river. It was not a choice he wanted to make. But it was the least bad choice.

Sullenberger recognized that a water landing, even in freezing temperatures, was a better (or less bad) option than the risk of fire, explosion, and loss of further life on the ground. While calm – admittedly, a forced calm – he made the tough call. It was an agonizing decision. But clear thinking, made possible by his forcing calm on himself, allowed him to make it.

Using his plane as a glider, he passed the George Washington Bridge at about 900 feet. He brought the plane down in a classic landing position, with the nose just above the tail, allowing the plane, in the words of one witness, to skim across the water like a flat pebble.

Captain Sullenberger not only made the right call on strategy – which choice to make – he also was able to execute the decision effectively, gliding his plane to a landing that didn't result in the aircraft coming apart, or sinking, or flipping over.

The 81-ton plane settled into the river, intact and afloat. The Hudson at the time was filled with ferries, small boats, and the usual Coast Guard, New York Police Department, and New York Fire Department watercraft. Within minutes the plane was surrounded by rescuers on boats, in helicopters, and in the case of NYPD rescue divers, in the water.

The 5-person flight crew kept the passengers calm and led an orderly evacuation. All 150 passengers, including a nine-month old baby, got out. One had two broken legs; others had impact injuries. And some had to be treated for hypothermia. The air temperature was about 30 degrees Fahrenheit; the water temperature close to freezing. But all the passengers, and all five crew, survived.

According to reports from the passengers and New York City Mayor Michael Bloomberg, once the passengers and other crew had evacuated Captain Sullenberger walked through the plane twice to assure that there was no one left.

One witness said that the back of the plane was filled with water to neck height. Captain Sullenberger was the last to climb into a raft. The last passenger to leave the plane told the news media that in the raft he gave the Captain a hug and called him "our hero."

New York State Governor David Paterson called the event "a miracle on the Hudson."

The next day, US Airways stock rose 15 percent, on a day when the market as a whole rose only a half of one percent.

The "Miracle on the Hudson" was not a miracle at all. It was the result of clear thinking, good choices, and effective execution.

Sullenberger is both a model of effective decision-making in a crisis and in many ways the exception.

Many leaders much of the time make poor choices in a crisis. Sometimes it is because they fail to take the crisis seriously until it is too late, an option not available to Sullenberger. Sometimes it is because they don't know how to choose (lack of intellectual rigor). And sometimes it is because they panic (lack of emotional discipline). All three of these failures can be traced to the leaders' failure to understand the dynamics that predictably lead to successful or unsuccessful outcomes (deep knowledge).

And sometimes leaders make poor choices because they think that the solution to a crisis is all about public relations.

Every Crisis is a Business Problem Before it is a Communication Problem

Crisis management is far more than skillful public relations. Seeing PR as the solution to a crisis is a recipe for failure.

Every crisis is a business problem before it is a communication problem, and leaders cannot communicate their way out of a business problem. They especially cannot communicate their way out of a problem they have behaved their way into. (Similarly, every crisis is a business problem before it's a legal problem.)

So the first task in effective crisis management is identifying and resolving the underlying business problem. Communication, when it is called for, describes the steps the company is taking to identify or resolve the problem, or expresses a commitment to doing so.

Indeed, there is an important role for effective communication as part of a larger crisis management process. (And also for good legal counsel.)

Crisis communication is a subset of crisis management that focuses on engaging stakeholders in order to maintain, restore, or enhance trust and confidence when something goes wrong.

Effective crisis communication is like what the military calls a "force multiplier." By itself it won't be sufficient to resolve the crisis and maintain trust and confidence; but when aligned with action it can help a company or leader accomplish more, better, and faster than without effective crisis communication.

By the time crises become public they play out in an environment of emotional resonance: fear, anxiety, anger, shame, embarrassment and other, often confused, emotions. Effective crisis communication, combined with effective management of other elements of a crisis, can address and even neutralize these emotional reactions.

Effective crisis response consists of a carefully managed process that calibrates smart actions with smart communication:

Crisis Response =

Effective Action + Effective Communication

But long before an organization engages its stakeholders it needs to make smart choices by asking the right questions and by following the right criteria.

Key Takeaways from This Chapter

The original word from which the English word *crisis* is derived was an ancient Greek word, *krisis* (κρισις). That word meant a decision or choice that a protagonist in a Greek tragedy had to make at a turning point that would determine his or her destiny. We remember those who chose poorly. We don't remember those who chose wisely.

Indeed, a wise choice would not be the topic of a Greek tragedy, the social media of its day.

The same applies in modern crises. We tend to remember those crises where leaders made poor choices. Stakeholders tend not to remember well-handled crises. And that's OK.

The classic on crisis decision-making is Steven Fink's 1986 *Crisis Management: Planning for the Inevitable.* In it Fink describes crises as a turning point, not necessarily a negative event of bad thing. He describes crises as "prodromal" – as precursors or predictors of something yet to come.

I believe that understanding crises in the Greek sense – as a moment of decision or choice in which one's destiny is determined – is the key to effective crisis management.

And as with any other management process, there is a rigor to getting it right.

That rigor includes understanding the problem by asking a sequence of questions intended to help make smart choices:

➢ Question 1: What do we have? Unless we name the problem accurately we will be unable to actually solve the problem quickly. There are several challenges in naming problem. First, there is a tendency to confuse a symptom of a problem for the problem itself (e.g. "We have a *60 Minutes* problem" rather than "We have an inappropriate business practice that is about to become public"). Sometimes the original description of the problem is based on confusion or lack of understanding.

Hence, General Motors mischaracterized a safety issue as a customer inconvenience, with fatal consequences.

➢ Question 2: What does it mean? Here we assess the significance of the problem. What are the likely consequences? How are the stakeholders who matter to us likely to react?

➢ Question 3: What do we want? We can't un-ring a bell, but we can consider the less bad outcome among the options available to   us.

➢ Question 4: How do we make the less bad outcome happen? How do we consider options and outcomes in such a way that we choose the less bad outcome? Too often leaders in crisis fail to consider options. But there's always more than one way to fix a problem. Or they choose among options based on personal preference or self-protection. When options don't immediately present themselves, we can project options based on magnitudes of response. Option 1: Do nothing out of the ordinary. Option 2: Do something small. Option 3: Do something   big.

The most productive way to choose among those options is to consider the options always in connection to the likely outcomes, both intended and unintended, positive and negative.

Sometimes the best choice is the choice with the least bad outcomes. It is not a choice we would want to make; but the consequences are less severe than the other options.

Sometimes leaders make poor choices because they think that crisis response is just an exercise in public relations. But seeing PR as the solution to a crisis is a recipe for failure.

Every crisis is a business problem before it is a communication problem. Crisis communication is a subset of crisis management that focuses on engaging stakeholders when trust, confidence, and other measures of competitive advantage are at risk.

But communication by itself is rarely enough. Effective crisis response calibrates smart action with smart communication.

Chapter 3:
Decision Criterion #1: What to Do?

Crisis management is the management of choices. And organizations that get through crises well tend to make smart choices at the right time.

But sometimes those choices can be quite scary. Sometimes the choices can be painful. And sometimes the prospect of this fear and pain causes leaders and organizations to make bad choices. They tend to make impulsive choices, and to make choices that are self-comforting. But these kinds of choices almost always make matters worse.

There's a kind of agony in having to make the decision. But the key to getting the decision right, to making decisions that actually resolve crises rather than intensify crises, is to think clearly. Or, as former CBS president and Dean of Columbia Journalism School Fred Friendly once said, the most productive way to escape the agony of decision is by thinking.

Thinking clearly to make smart choices requires using the right decision criteria – the proper basis for choice. That means asking the right questions to understand the actual problem and its significance. And it means understanding the options to consider, and the likely consequences of each option.

But at its heart making smart choices means asking the right questions.

The significance of asking the right questions was brought to light by Albert Einstein, winner of the Nobel Prize in Physics and *Time* magazine's Man of the Century for the Twenty-First Century, who observed,

> If I had an hour to solve a problem and my life depended on the solution, I would spend the first 55 minutes determining the proper question to ask, for once I know the proper question, I could solve the problem in less than five minutes.[39]

Indeed, in my experience working on and studying thousands of crises over more than 35 years, the most effectively handled crises were the ones where the solution could be figured out quickly because the right questions were asked. Ask the right question, and the solution can become clear within a matter of minutes. But asking the right question requires mental readiness: emotional discipline, deep knowledge, and intellectual rigor. And also a readiness to shift perspective and to think differently.

In a crisis, business as usual has ceased to exist. The American sociologist Tamotsu Shibutani defines a crisis as:

> any situation in which the previously established social machinery breaks down, a point at which some kind of readjustment is required... A crisis is a crisis precisely because [people] cannot act effectively together. When previously accepted norms prove inadequate guides for conduct, a situation becomes problematic, and some kind of emergency action is required. Since activity is temporarily blocked, a sense of frustration arises; if the crisis persists, tension mounts, and an increasing sense of urgency for doing something develops.[40]

The leadership discipline is to recognize that in a business-other-than-usual environment leaders need to think differently.

Precisely because business as usual no longer applies, the usual decision processes or frames of reference will not work. Effective leaders condition their minds to be ready to think differently when circumstances require. This mental readiness, this ability to see a situation from a different frame of reference than usual, is a key leadership discipline.

Criteria matter. Most leaders, much of the time, apply the wrong criteria because they ask themselves the wrong question. And they ask the wrong question because they're thinking in the wrong way. Again, per Einstein, "No problem can be solved by the same kind of thinking that created it."[41] Rather, we need to change the frame of reference in which a crisis response is considered.

Asking the Wrong Questions

Most counter-productive crisis responses begin with leaders asking some version of *What should we do?* Even more counterproductive is to start with *What should we say?*

The challenge with this kind of question is that it focuses on the **we** – on the entity or leader in crisis. This results in the consideration of options that may make the people in midst of crisis feel good – Let's do this! or Let's say this! But this kind of question is unlikely to lead to options that succeed in maintaining the trust, confidence, and support of those people whose trust, confidence, and support are critical to the company.

Many leaders, much of the time, tend to see the world from the point of view of their own operations, and are unaware of any other way to see the world. They suffer from the curse of knowledge – where they know so much about their topic that they can't conceive of people not knowing what they're talking about. But stakeholders don't see the world in the same way that organizations do. They don't care about internal operations, and they don't need to understand those operations to be in relation with a company or its leaders. But they do care about how the organization can affect them, positively or negatively.

Netflix and Self-Referential Communication

A good example of this kind of failure is Netflix' mishandling of a relatively routine change in service offering and price. Until the summer of 2011 Netflix offered customers a joint plan that allowed them to rent DVDs by mail, one at a time, plus unlimited streaming of video programming. Each kind of video had different content choices, and could be experienced differently – for example, an Internet connection is required for streaming, but not for DVD.

In July, 2011 Neflix announced a change through an email from the head of marketing to Netflix' customers. It said that there would be two new DVD-only plans, a one-at-a-time plan for $7.99 per month, and a two-at-a-time plan for $11.99.[11] The email emphasized that these were the lowest prices ever for unlimited DVDs. So far, so good.

The next paragraph, however, left people initially confused:

> Second, we are separating unlimited DVDs by mail and unlimited streaming into separate plans to better reflect the costs of each and to give our members a choice: a streaming only plan, a DVD only plan or the option to subscribe to both.

With this change, we will no longer offer a plan that includes both unlimited streaming and DVDs by mail.[42]

That somewhat dense paragraph wasn't particularly easy to follow. What did it mean to no longer offer a plan that includes both unlimited streaming and DVD by mail? Were they canceling something, or simply not taking new customers? It wasn't clear. The next paragraph, where one would expect an explanation, was about price. And it made people angry:

> So for instance, our current $9.99 a month membership for unlimited streaming and unlimited DVDs will be split into 2 distinct plans:
>
> Plan 1: Unlimited Streaming (no DVDs) for $7.99 a month.
>
> Plan 2: Unlimited DVDs, 1 out at-a-time (no streaming), for $7.99 a month.
>
> The price for getting both of these plans will be $15.98 a month ($7.99 + $7.99). For new members, these changes are effective immediately; for existing members, the new pricing will start for charges on or after September 1, 2011.[43]

In other words, customers had to choose: Give up DVDs, give up streaming, or pay $15.98 a month for bundled service that previously cost only $9.99. A price increase of 60 percent. But the magnitude of that increase wasn't made explicit in the e-mail. Customers had to do the math themselves. And it came with an added inconvenience: Instead of a single bundled plan, customers would need to maintain two separate plans. Without any discount for having both.

But the longest section of the note was the explanation. And it wasn't satisfying. It spoke about the company's operations, the company's concerns about the viability of the DVD business, and an internal company reorganization:

> Why the changes?
>
> Last November when we launched our $7.99 unlimited streaming plan, DVDs by mail was treated as a $2 add on to our unlimited streaming plan. At the time, we didn't anticipate offering DVD only plans. Since then we have realized that there is still a very large continuing demand for DVDs both from our existing members as well as non-members. Given the long life we think DVDs by mail will have, treating DVDs as a $2 add on to our unlimited streaming plan neither makes great financial sense nor satisfies people who just want DVDs. Creating an unlimited DVDs by mail plan (no streaming) at our lowest price ever, $7.99, does make sense and will ensure a long life for our DVDs by mail offering. Reflecting our confidence that DVDs by mail is a long-term business for us, we are also establishing a separate and distinct management team solely focused on DVDs by mail, led by Andy Rendich, our Chief Service and Operations Officer and an 11 year veteran of Netflix.
>
> Now we offer a choice: Unlimited Streaming for $7.99 a month, Unlimited DVDs for $7.99 a month, or both for $15.98 a month ($7.99 + $7.99). We think $7.99 is a terrific value for our unlimited streaming plan and $7.99 a terrific value for our unlimited DVD plan. We hope one, or both, of these plans makes sense for our members and their entertainment needs.[44]

What was remarkable about that explanation is that it was all framed from the perspective of the company. Not about customers, or about customer desires, behavior, or preferences. Nothing about customer convenience, ensuring quality service, or broadening the selection. It was all about the internal operations of Netflix and its view of the viability of its DVD business.

It was as if the company didn't care about its customers' likely reaction. There was no acknowledgment of any inconvenience to customers, or even of an all-in price increase. It was an exercise in corporate-speak, not in human connection. And instead of closing with an expression of gratitude for the customers' loyalty, the note simply said,

> As always, our members can easily choose to change or cancel their unlimited streaming plan, unlimited DVD plan, or both by visiting Your Account.[45]

Many chose to cancel. Presented with an apparent take-it-or-leave-it choice, it was easy for customers, especially those who had a negative emotional reaction, to simply click on the link and cancel.

Within hours social media was flooded with customer complaints. The company's own blog saw more than 12,000 comments. Most were very negative. Some were angry.

The news media quickly seized upon the story, with ample coverage of customers' angry reaction. The stock market also reacted. While the stock rose a bit immediately after the announcement, to just about $300 per share, within two months – as investors began to recognize the financial impact of customer defections – the stock had fallen by a third, to $200.

All the while, Netflix was silent, as customers continued to criticize and abandon the company in the run-up to the September 1st price increase.

Netflix fell into a trap many companies and leaders often find hard to avoid: It communicated at its stakeholders, not with them. Its leaders saw the world through the perspective of their own operations, and simply conveyed their business decision to stakeholders using their own frame of reference.

But that frame of reference almost never succeeds in winning stakeholders' hearts and minds, especially when there's a potentially negative impact on them. In other words, they asked *What should we say?* And the predictable outcome of framing the event from their own perspective is that they alienated their customers.

The crisis guru, and my dear friend and mentor, James E. Lukaszewski, in a gem of a book called *Influencing Public Attitudes,* notes that audiences typically don't care about a company's operations. They don't have sympathy for the business challenges or logistical issues a company may face. They care only about the impact on them. Lukaszewski says that audiences don't care because they can't care. Audiences don't know – and don't want or need to know – about a company's internal operations. To get an audience to care, a company and its leaders need to begin with the audience's concerns and then link those concerns to what the company is doing.[19]

For leaders who live and breathe the company's operations, this common-sense observation is hard to grasp. Stakeholders have their own ideas, their own concerns, their own frames of reference. And if we want to maintain their trust and confidence, we need to start by taking those ideas, concerns, and frames of reference seriously.

Netflix framed its communication with customers in the voice of the marketing vice president, who spoke about the changes in the service Netflix would provide, and the new pricing, without acknowledging the inconvenience to the customers.

In the process, Netflix failed to anticipate the emotional reaction its customers had – both to the price increase and to the manner in which it was conveyed. And Netflix seemed to be blindsided by the anger.

Netflix was silent for the next two months. Then, on September 18th Netflix customers received an even more curious e-mail, this time from Netflix CEO Reed Hastings. His note was also posted on the company's blog, along with a video version. Hastings began by acknowledging Netflix's missteps in the July announcement:

> I messed up. I owe you an explanation.
>
> It is clear from the feedback over the past two months that many members felt we lacked respect and humility in the way we announced the separation of DVD and streaming and the price changes. That was certainly not our intent, and I offer my sincere apology.[46]

It was a good beginning. It came from the top of the company. It acknowledged that Netflix was listening to customer feedback. It noted that customers were angry with the company. And his apology seemed (so far) to be sincere.

Then he went on to give an explanation, first about the nature of the July announcement. He noted the need to adapt quickly to a changing market, and made reference to two companies that had been pioneers but had not been able to adapt. One, Borders, a large brick-and-mortar bookstore, had gone out of business earlier that year. His point seemed to be that, to continue to survive, Netflix needed to evolve beyond its initial business model. He didn't say it outright, but that was a reasonable interpretation of his explanation:

> Let me explain what we are doing.
>
> For the past five years, my greatest fear at Netflix has been that we wouldn't make the leap from success in DVDs to success in streaming. Most companies that are great at something — like AOL dialup or Borders bookstores — do not become great at new things people want (streaming for us). So we moved quickly into streaming, but I should have personally given you a full explanation of why we are splitting the services and thereby increasing prices. It wouldn't have changed the price increase, but it would have been the right thing to do.[47]

Hastings noted that the price increase would have been necessary in any event. And he acknowledged his failure to give an appropriate explanation of the reasons. His e-mail continued:

> So here is what we are doing and why.
>
> Many members love our DVD service, as I do, because nearly every movie ever made is published on DVD. DVD is a great option for those who want the huge and comprehensive selection of movies.
>
> I also love our streaming service because it is integrated into my TV, and I can watch anytime I want. The benefits of our streaming service are really quite different from the benefits of DVD by mail. We need to focus on rapid improvement as streaming technology and the market evolves, without maintaining compatibility with our DVD by mail service.
>
> So we realized that streaming and DVD by mail are really becoming two different businesses, with very different cost structures, that need to be marketed differently, and we need to let each grow and operate independently.[48]

The key new insight in his explanation is the recognition that the dynamics of the two forms of video delivery – physical DVDs by mail, and streaming video via the Internet – were diverging into separate businesses.

But as in the July announcement, the explanation was all about the company. He didn't explain what he meant by the "need to focus on rapid improvement as streaming technology and the market evolves, without maintaining compatibility with our DVD by mail service." He may have meant the desire to provide faster downloads, greater selection, greater product variety, or any manner of things customers might care about. But it seemed to be just more corporate-speak.

But the next three paragraphs went well beyond explaining the July decision. Rather, they offered a stunning new piece of information. The company would split in two:

> It's hard to write this after over 10 years of mailing DVDs with pride, but we think it is necessary: In a few weeks, we will rename our DVD by mail service to "Qwikster." We chose the name Qwikster because it refers to quick delivery. We will keep the name "Netflix" for streaming.
>
> Qwikster will be the same website and DVD service that everyone is used to. It is just a new name, and DVD members will go to qwikster.com to access their DVD queues and choose movies. One improvement we will make at launch is to add a video games upgrade option, similar to our upgrade option for Blu-ray, for those who want to rent Wii, PS3 and Xbox 360 games. Members have been asking for video games for many years, but now that DVD by mail has its own team, we are finally getting it done. Other improvements will follow. A negative of the renaming and separation is that the Qwikster.com and Netflix.com websites will not be integrated.

There are no pricing changes (we're done with that!). If you subscribe to both services you will have two entries on your credit card statement, one for Qwikster and one for Netflix. The total will be the same as your current charges. We will let you know in a few weeks when the Qwikster.com website is up and ready.[49]

Unstated in that explanation, "Qwikster.com and Netflix.com websites will not be integrated," was a new wrinkle for those customers who still wanted to maintain both DVD and streaming video service: Not only would they be paying more than previously, but now they would need to log into two separate websites and maintain two separate accounts. And the stated reason seemed to be merely the difference in name of the two different delivery options. Customers weighing the inconvenience against the stated reason – the new name – didn't understand how the trade-off benefited them. Hastings closed by reaching out to his customers:

I want to acknowledge and thank you for sticking with us, and to apologize again to those members, both current and former, who felt we treated them thoughtlessly.

Both the Qwikster and Netflix teams will work hard to regain your trust. We know it will not be overnight. Actions speak louder than words. But words help people to understand actions.

Respectfully yours,

-Reed Hastings, Co-Founder and CEO, Netflix.[50]

Rather than resolve customer concerns, Hastings's letter only made matters worse. Although he had apologized for treating customers thoughtlessly in the July announcement, many customers thought this letter was even more thoughtless, and they had an even worse reaction. As in July, this e-mail was framed from the company's perspective: the split between DVDs and streaming were described in language about the company's business model. It didn't acknowledge the impact of the two separate services on customers. Customers were not amused. But Netflix again seemed surprised by their reaction.

The media covered the current wave of customer anger and revisited the initial July backlash, including the fact that hundreds of thousands of customers had canceled their membership.

The next day *Investor's Business Daily* newspaper covered both Netflix customers' anger and its investors' puzzlement. The story, by Patrick Seitz, headlined "Netflix Tries Damage Control; Qwikster Doesn't Help," began,

> Netflix on Monday apologized for angering customers over a recent price increase, then turned around and angered them once more by splitting its DVD and streaming video business.[51]

Several days later *New York Times* technology columnist David Pogue captured the mood of his fellow Netflix customers. Pogue recounted how ten years earlier he had written a column praising Netflix, but how the company's recent stumbles had caused him to reconsider. Writing about his initial praise, he said:

> The best part is the conclusion of that column, where I called Netflix "a shining example of a dot-com that's still in business because it's an indisputable consumer win, not just a greed play.
> O.K., I stand corrected.[52]

Pogue then cataloged his and other Netflix customers' disappointment:

> In July, Netflix enraged its 25 million customers by abruptly jacking up the price of its DVD plus streaming-movies plan by 60 percent – from $10 a month to $16.
>
> When I wrote about the turnabout, I noted that the most frustrating part was the incomprehensible explanation that Netflix provided…
>
> In any case, Netflix subscribers were furious. In a matter of weeks, one million of them canceled their memberships.
>
> So a few days ago, Reed Hastings, Netflix's chief executive, sent Netflix members an e-mail message that got off to a good start. Mine read:
>
> 'Dear David, I messed up. I owe you an explanation.
>
> 'It is clear from the feedback over the past two months that many members felt we lacked respect and humility in the way we announced the separation of DVD and streaming and the price changes. That was certainly not our intent, and I offer my sincere apology. Let me explain what we are doing.'
>
> Ah. O.K., good. We've seen this movie before. Corporation bumbles, apologizes, makes things right. Business schools take note. Life goes on.
>
> But this time, Mr. Hastings did not follow the formula. He only pretended to.[53]

Pogue then highlighted the customer service consequences of splitting the DVD service into Qwikster and the streaming service into Netflix: the need to visit two separate websites, maintain two accounts, pay two separate credit card bills; view separate movie catalogs; deal with two different order lists – in other words, lots of inconvenience for the customer, all the while costing more.[54]

Pogue closed his column by criticizing Netflix's leadership:

I confess: I'm utterly baffled.

At why Netflix, long hailed for its masterfully gracious customer focus, has suddenly become tone-deaf to the effects of its clumsy elephant-in-a-china-shop maneuvers.

At the reasons behind all of these shenanigans. Yes, of course, fewer people use DVDs, but come on, they haven't all fallen off a cliff simultaneously.

At why Mr. Hastings thinks it helps to say "I messed up" without actually making things right. That's one of the hollowest apologies I've ever heard. It's lip service. It's like the politician who says, "I'm sorry you feel that way." You're not sorry—in fact, you're still insisting that you're right.

In the end, though, what makes me unhappiest is how calculated all of this feels....

Yes, Mr. Hastings, you did mess up. Twice.[55]

Netflix's stock fell on the news. It had been at $300 just after the July announcement; it was at $233 on September 1st. By October 1st it had fallen to $113. In other words, Netflix stock had lost nearly two-thirds of its market value since the July announcement.

Then on October 10th, just three weeks after announcing the split, a chastened Reed Hastings sent an e-mail to customers (also posted on the company blog). It was not expansive; it offered little explanation or apology. But in it Hastings reversed course. The very brief e-mail began:

It is clear that for many of our members two websites would make things more difficult, so we are going to keep Netflix as one place to go for streaming and DVDs.

This means no change: one website, one account, one password...in other words, no Qwikster.

While the July price change was necessary, we are now done with price changes.[56]

There was then a single paragraph about increases in the offerings of several movie and TV production studios.[31] Hastings closed with this:

> We value our members, and we are committed to making Netflix the best place to get movies & TV shows.
> Thank you.
> -Reed[57]

The move was welcomed by some customers. But there was also anger at Hastings.

The stock continued its slide, and closed at $78 in late October, and under $70 in late November, from $300 just after the July 12th announcement. In other words, a loss of market value of nearly 75 percent. And the defection of more than a million customers. And some meaningful resentment and mistrust among many remaining customers.

Netflix is a good example of the appreciation of Fink's definition of crisis. It isn't something bad that has already happened. Rather, it's a turning point moment, what Fink calls "prodromal," a precursor to something yet to come, that can go one way or the other.

But Netflix failed to see the risk in that turning point moment. And it stayed in its own frame of reference, and seemed to have asked itself only, *What do we say about the service and price change?* But by asking the question that way about themselves, they failed to address legitimate customer concerns.

What is needed is a different kind of thinking that begins not with the *I/me/we/us* but rather with the **they/them** – with the stakeholders who matter to the organization. The leadership discipline of mental readiness – the readiness to shift frames of reference from the first person – *I/me/we/us* -- to the third person – **they/them** – makes all the difference.

And that's because of the way trust works.

Maintaining Trust

One goal for most organizations and leaders in crises is to maintain the trust and confidence of those who matter – shareholders, employees, customers, regulators, etc.

Trust arises when stakeholders' legitimate expectations are met. Trust falls when expectations are unmet.

Asking *What should we do?* runs the serious risk of failing even to consider stakeholders' expectations. Worse, it further risks the leader becoming stuck in his or her own perspective, in **I/me/we/us**. Hence, such crisis whoppers as President Richard Nixon's "I am not a crook," and even BP CEO Tony Hayward's "What the hell did we do to deserve this [criticism]"? followed soon after by "I'd like my life back," which we'll explore in greater detail later in this chapter.

Many crisis response failures can be traced back to the ultimate decision-makers focusing on their own frame of reference rather than on victims or other stakeholders. This was the pattern, for example, in the way the Church hierarchy handled pedophile priests for decades in the Roman Catholic clergy child sex abuse crisis. They found ways to protect the priests, not the children. This began to change after 2003, but that change was slow (See Chapter 5 for more on the Catholic Church crisis).

The best description of trust that I have found is from Frank Navran, for years a principal consultant to the Ethics Resource Center in Washington. He writes, "Trust is the natural consequence of promises fulfilled." Says Navran, "Trust results from having one's expectations met, of having no unrealized expectations (what we refer to as disappointments)."[58]

So the most productive way to maintain trust in a crisis is to fulfill the legitimate expectations of those who matter.

Because trust is the consequence of expectations fulfilled, the right question to ask when determining the appropriate course of action in a crisis is not *What should we do?* Or *What should we say?* Rather, think of the stakeholders who matter to your organization. Then, with those stakeholders in mind, ask:

What would reasonable people appropriately expect a responsible organization or leader to do when facing this kind of situation?

Framing decisions in light of stakeholder expectations leads to smarter choices faster, and maintains stakeholders' trust.

But the discipline – the rigor – of asking the right question is just the start. There needs to be equivalent rigor in all the ways that question is interpreted and answered. For example, the question itself has several variables:

➢ *Reasonable* people: The word *reasonable* is quite subjective. What may be reasonable to one person may be unreasonable to others.

But we already have precedents in understanding reasonableness that most leaders and complex organizations are familiar with. For example, in the financial markets the U.S. Securities and Exchange Commission requires companies to disclose information that a "reasonable investor" would consider important in making an investment decision. And the U.S. Federal Trade Commission says that for an advertisement to be considered deceptive "the representation, omission or practice must be likely to mislead reasonable consumers under the circumstances."[59]

So we already have frameworks for determining reasonableness in our stakeholders. Just as we need the intellectual rigor to see crises not merely from our own perspective, we need also further to see the crisis from the perspective of reasonable stakeholders, not unreasonable stakeholders.

For example, in the immediate aftermath of an explosion or fire, reasonable stakeholders would not expect an organization to know the precise cause of the explosion or fire. Media will inquire, and social media will speculate, but no trust will be lost simply because the organization doesn't immediately know or disclose the cause. Similarly, if there have been fatalities reasonable people don't appropriately expect a responsible organization to disclose the names of the dead before family members have been notified. Again, media will ask, and social media will speculate. But media inquiry and social media speculation do not define what is reasonable. And trust will not fall just because the organization waited to be sure family members knew before the names were publicly disclosed.

➢ *Appropriate* expectations: Similarly, reasonable stakeholders would not appropriately expect a company to immediately fire someone just because they have been accused of misconduct.

But they would expect the company to take the accusation seriously and to investigate both quickly and thoroughly and to take steps based on the findings, including potentially firing the employee. And if the accusation was that the employee put others at risk, the appropriate expectation would be that the employee be removed from the environment while the investigation is under way.

➢ *Responsible* organization or leader: The most challenging aspect of mental readiness is seen in the third of these concepts, the notion of what reasonable stakeholders would appropriately expect a <u>responsible</u> organization or leader to do.

Notice that the question is not asked about the leader's actual organization. I find that considering the actual organization as a first resort is counterproductive. It keeps things in *I/me/we/us* mode. One result is that people filter out common sense solutions – *We'd never get approval for that* or *We can't get budget for that* or *We tried something like that before and it didn't work* – and so they don't even offer solutions.

In client meetings during a crisis I often see such a dynamic taking place. My approach is to redirect the discussion. I say, *Forget about us; assume we work in a responsible organization – that could be us, or it could be someone else. And assume this kind of crisis. What would reasonable people appropriately expect a responsible organization like us to do when facing this kind of crisis?*

I have asked this question of companies large and small; of religious denominations; of universities; of military commands. And in each instance the question prompts a much more robust list of options, all of which are more likely to be helpful. I then go down the list: *Can we do this one? This one? This one?* And we end up with much more productive recommendations.

Applying Decision Criterion #1

For any stakeholder group we can answer the question, *What would reasonable people appropriately expect a responsible organization or leader to do?* to a very granular level.

We can inventory expectations to the level of a large universe, such as all employees or of a much narrower universe, such as those hourly unionized employees on the second shift of a certain factory; to the level of all regulators or of only those regulators at a particular regulatory agency; to the level of a broad universe such as all customers or of a narrower universe such as all customers who bought a certain product at a certain retailer on a certain day.

And we can then work to fulfill those specific expectations.

There are a number of ways to identify expectations with confidence. For example, if there are legal or regulatory requirements, reasonable people would appropriately expect a responsible organization to meet its legal and regulatory requirements. Does the company have a statement of values, a brand promise, or code of ethics? Reasonable people appropriately expect a responsible organization to fulfill the expectations that the organization itself has set.

Once an expectation is set, the organization must either fulfill the expectation or reset it, or risk disappointment that shatters trust.

Resetting an expectation may cause some short-term pain. But it's preferable to wholesale disappointment. Take a relatively trivial example: You're running late for a meeting. The meeting is the expectation – that you'll arrive at a certain place at a certain time to meet with someone. If you're 20 minutes late, the person waiting for you will be rightly disappointed, and may form a very negative impression. But if before the appointed time you call ahead and say you're running late, you'll get the benefit of the doubt. You will have reset the expectation. The person may still be disappointed, but less so, and for different reasons.

The same applies to big, complex expectations. Ideally, the leader sets an appropriate expectation and avoids saying what merely sounds good but is unlikely to be fulfilled. And when circumstances change, the leader can adapt to those changes and recalibrate the expectations.

But whether with an initial expectation or a recalibrated expectation, if a leader or organization wants to maintain trust, the promises must come true. It's not enough to say, "We'll be there for you." The leader's organization must actually be there.

The Common Expectation: Care

Regardless the particular expectations of any given stakeholder group, there is a common expectation that applies to all stakeholder groups all the time: In a crisis, all stakeholders expect a responsible organization or leader to care. To care that something has happened; to care that people need help; to care that something needs to be done.

One of the common patterns in crisis is this: The single biggest predictor of loss of trust and confidence, of loss of reputation, and of financial and operational harm, is the perception that the organization or leader does not care.

So effective crisis response, at a minimum, begins with a timely demonstration of caring. And it continues with a persistent demonstration that the organization and leader continue to care, for as long as the expectation of caring exists.

What it takes to show we care may vary across time – what it takes to show we care early in a crisis will be different from later in the crisis. And it will vary across stakeholder groups and across types of crises. But that we need to show we care will not change.

Showing we care is not sentimental. It is a leadership discipline; it is part of mental readiness to do what is necessary to protect trust and confidence in a crisis.

Anything that detracts from the perception that the organization or its leader cares diminishes trust and confidence in the aftermath of a crisis.

The crisis guru Jim Lukaszewski, in *Lukaszewski on Crisis Communication: What Your CEO Needs to Know About Reputation Risk and Crisis Management*, says that the principal ingredient of any crisis is the creation of victims. Caring about the victims becomes key.

> Crisis-created internal and external victims are the greatest threat to the organization. A key role for senior management, as well as other managers, is making certain that the needs of victims are tended to immediately, fully and compassionately. The most significant causes of litigation and lousy visibility during crises are the ignored or discredited needs of victims, victims' families, and survivors—and the failure of leadership to aggressively manage the victim dimension.[60]

Lukaszewski notes that managing the victim dimension – attending to the needs of victims, and of those who empathize with victims – is the key to maintaining reputation, trust, and confidence.

He explains that while victimhood is a self-designated and self-sustaining state, it is also a self-terminating state. Victims stop feeling like victims when companies offer simple, sincere, and positive responses to their plight. He notes:

> Actions, communications, and behaviors that fail to meet these three challenging standards will fail by prolonging the victimization.[61]

BP and the Failure to Show It Cared

We can see the principles described so far in the case of Tony Hayward, the chief executive officer of BP in 2010.

On April 20th, 2010 the Deepwater Horizon oil rig, an off-shore drilling platform operated by BP, exploded. Eleven employees were killed in the explosion and subsequent fire; dozens were injured. The explosion led to a gush of oil from the base of the well about five miles under the surface in the Gulf of Mexico.

Note that this was not a leak — the gradual emission of a finite amount of material — nor a spill — a more rapid loss of a finite amount of material. Rather, it was a gush — an uncontrolled, continuous release of crude oil under high pressure from deep under the surface of the water. By the time the well was fully capped, on September 19th, more than 4.9 million barrels — 780 million gallons — of crude oil had been released into the Gulf.

In a crisis management seminar I teach in New York University's Stern School of Business Executive MBA program, I ask students to act as the crisis response team for BP in the early hours of the crisis.

They follow the Understand the Problem questions from Chapter 2 to get a good sense of the situation. I then ask them to consider the question of what BP should do: **What would reasonable people among BP's stakeholder groups appropriately expect a responsible petroleum extraction company to do when one of its rigs explodes?**

The answers are always consistent, and include

➤ Take care of the families of those killed.

➤ Take care of the injured employees and their families.

➤ Make sure others who worked on the rig are ok, physically and emotionally.

➤ Know how to prevent environmental harm, and then actually prevent it.

➤ Know how to clean up and repair any environmental damage, and then clean it up and repair it.

➤ Suspend operations on other rigs until the cause of the explosion is known.

And in terms of communication, the answers include:

➤ Express remorse for your employees who were killed.

➤ Express remorse and commitment to care for the employees who were injured.

➤ Express a commitment to protect people and the environment.

➤ Express a commitment to the uninterrupted flow of product to customers.

Those actions and communications, individually and collectively, would have the effect of demonstrating that BP cared.

But BP did not do those things.

BP was not mentally ready, nor operationally ready, to deal with the aftermath of the explosion. Plans that BP had submitted to regulators were later found to have been unrealistically and misleadingly optimistic of their capacities to deal with the release of oil into the Gulf. Hayward later admitted that BP was making it up as they went along.[62]

The oil continued gushing despite many failed attempts to control the well over a five month period, ultimately creating the single worst environmental disaster in American history.[63]

And BP's early crisis communication response seemed to be based on asking the question, *What should we say?* BP persisted in saying things that made themselves feel better. But their statements predictably caused others to question both their competence and their integrity.

About a week after the rig exploded, Hayward was quoted in *The New York Times* from an internal meeting where after describing the criticism BP had suffered he asked, "What the hell did we do to deserve this?"[64] A recording of the meeting leaked, and went viral.

Stakeholders took the statement as an expression of self-pity for the criticism the company was receiving because of its inability to control the well. They perceived that BP didn't care about the victims of the explosion, only about themselves.

A few days later Hayward, speaking of the contractor whose rig BP had hired to explore for oil, said,

> This was not our accident. This was not our drilling rig...This was not our equipment. It was not our people, our systems or our processes. This was Transocean's rig. Their systems. Their people. Their equipment.[65]

While technically a true statement, BP, as the contracting company, was both legally responsible and publicly seen to be the owner of the well site. The statement was interpreted as an attempt to shift blame and attention from BP to its contractor. And, again, as a failure to care about the victims.

About ten days after that, Hayward was quoted in the *Guardian* newspaper saying,

> The Gulf of Mexico is a very big ocean. The amount of volume of oil and dispersant we are putting into it is tiny in relation to the total water volume.[66]

While technically true, the statement came after three weeks of continuous coverage of the spill and its environmental impact, and as waves were carrying the oil onto the beaches of Louisiana, Alabama, and Mississippi. The statement was interpreted as further proof that BP didn't care and that it didn't understand or even acknowledge the public's appropriate concerns about the environmental damage and its aftermath on marine life, fisheries, tourism, and the local economy in general.

The final defining moment in BP's CEO's public commentary came on May 30th, forty days after the spill, and after significant criticism that the company and its leaders didn't care.

Hayward held a press conference on a dock on the Louisiana coast. He tried to explain that he did care. He apologized for the impact the spill had on residents of the Gulf, and he tried to show that his interests were aligned with the Gulf residents' interests:

> I'm sorry. We're very sorry for the massive disruption that it has caused to their lives. There's no one who wants this over more than I do. You know, I'd like my life back.[67]

The first part of the statement was fine, if forty days late. But the last sentence, wanting his life back, did not work. He clearly meant it as metaphor. But critics pounced and pointed out that 11 rig workers who had died could never have their lives back; that those injured would have their lives changed forever; that residents of the Gulf had their livelihoods affected in meaningful ways. It was the beginning of the end for Hayward. He lost the trust and confidence of those who mattered most to him, including senior officials in the U.S. government and, eventually, of his own board of directors. He was out of a job several months later.

Of course, BP's problem was far bigger than failing to show it cared after the rig exploded. At its heart the whole Deepwater Horizon incident itself stemmed from a failure to care. In both the planning to bring the rig online and the planning for what could go wrong, BP seemed to go through the motions and not to consider the real possibility of failure.

For example, a National Academy of Engineering investigation concluded in November 2010 that BP and its contractors missed and ignored warning signs before the blowout and showed an "insufficient consideration of risk." The Associated Press reported:

Those failures would be unacceptable in companies that work with nuclear power or aviation, said Donald Winter, a professor of engineering practice at the University of Michigan and chairman of the 15-member study committee. 'A great number of decisions, all of which appear to us to be questionable … also appeared to be justified by those individuals and those companies involved,' Winter said Wednesday in an interview with The Associated Press. 'In an operation like this you have to recognize the uncertainties of where you are going.'[68]

Indeed, Donald Winter, the committee's chairman, told the *New York Times* that it appeared that measures were taken at least in part to save time and money. The troubled well was already behind schedule and costing BP $1.5 million per day.

> 'That gives us concern that there was not proper consideration of the tradeoffs between cost and schedule and risk and safety,' he said in a telephone interview.[69]

Among the tradeoffs, according to the *Washington Post*, was skimping on materials and equipment that industry standards prescribe for assuring the integrity of the well. The newspaper wrote, in advance of a congressional hearing about the explosion, that emails showed that:

> Four days before the April 20 explosion… one of BP's operations drilling engineers, sent an e-mail to a colleague noting that engineers had not taken all the usual steps to center the steel pipe in the drill hole, a standard procedure designed to ensure that the pipe would be properly cemented in place. '[W]ho cares, it's done, end of story, will probably be fine and we'll get a good cement job,' he wrote.[70]

That decision was about the number of centralizers that would assure that the pipe was properly aligned in the well hole. Halliburton, the contractor assigned to out cement and the pipe wall had planned to use 21 such centralizers. The *Washington Post* reports,

> Halliburton warned that without the full complement of centralizers, the danger of cracks in the cement surrounding the pipe increased. The American Petroleum Institute's recommended practices say that if the pipe, or casing, is not centered, 'it is difficult, if not impossible,' for the cement to displace the drilling mud on the narrow side of the opening. That could create channels for gas to travel up the well.
>
> But the equipment needed to center the well in all 21 places was not on the rig. A BP rig worker located some pieces in Houston and made arrangements to fly them to the rig, but more senior officials decided against doing so. In an e-mail April 16, BP's well team leader [John] Guide said that 'it will take 10 hours to install them. . . . I do not like this,' according to [a letter to BP by congressmen Henry Waxman (D-CA) and Bart Stupak (D-MI)].
>
> That sentiment reflected a pattern of time-and money-saving measures, Waxman and Stupak wrote. They said their investigation is "raising serious questions" about decisions made in the days and hours before the explosion on the drilling rig that sank. According to the committee's investigation, other decisions also "posed a tradeoff between cost and safety."[71]

Similarly, BP was obligated by law to file oil spill response plans with the federal government assuring that it had the capacity to respond to a worst-case discharge in the event of a rig accident. Soon after the explosion the Associated Press investigated those plans. According to CBS News:

> Professor Peter Lutz is listed in BP's 2009 response plan for a Gulf of Mexico oil spill as a national wildlife expert. He died in 2005.
>
> Under the heading 'sensitive biological resources,' the plan lists

marine mammals including walruses, sea otters, sea lions and seals. None lives anywhere near the Gulf.

The names and phone numbers of several Texas A&M University marine life specialists are wrong. So are the numbers for marine mammal stranding network offices in Louisiana and Florida, which are no longer in service.

BP PLC's 582-page regional spill plan for the Gulf, and its 52-page, site-specific plan for the Deepwater Horizon rig are riddled with omissions and glaring errors, according to an Associated Press analysis that details how BP officials have pretty much been making it up as they go along. The lengthy plans approved by the federal government last year before BP drilled its ill-fated well vastly understate the dangers posed by an uncontrolled leak and vastly overstate the company's preparedness to deal with one.[72]

The overwhelming conclusion from BP's involvement in the Deepwater Horizon well, from the immediate reaction to the explosion, to the process by which the explosion took place, to the purported plans to deal with a worst-case incident, is that BP seemed not to care.

To be sure, even as the public was reacting negatively to BP's ineffective response, BP was doing a number of things to help mitigate the damage to individuals. In addition to paying billions in fines and penalties later, during the crisis BP also distributed billions of dollars for things they didn't have to do.

BP helped people in affected communities make house payments; they replaced fishermen's commission payments on fish that were never harvested, and helped with boat payments. Thousands of people were hired in every state to more or less stand on the shore waiting for the oil to arrive and to rescue animals.

BP sold 20 percent of the company to finance an historic $30 billion damage pre-payment fund administered by a special master. That special master distributed the funds to those who had claims against BP. But in this process there were no attorneys allowed, so the recipients got 100 percent of what was awarded them. The trial bar is still spending tremendous energy and resources to bust this idea to pieces.

The company also made voluntary payments in the millions, to supplement individual state economic development communication and remediation from the damage. It launched a whole series of websites and dashboards that are still available from their archives to permit real-time and historical monitoring of what was going on. Much of this was put in place while Hayward was at the helm.

But because of its own operational and communication missteps, BP got no credit for this work.

The consequences were considerable.

In the end, BP pleaded guilty to eleven counts of manslaughter, to two misdemeanors, and to one felony count of lying to Congress. BP paid out more than $62 billion in fines, clean-up costs, settlements, and payments to the government. BP's stock fell from $60.57 on the day before the explosion to $29.20 on the day Hayward left BP, a loss of $105 billion. As this book is going to press, in June of 2017, BP stock is at $36.00, down about 40 percent from the pre-explosion price. In the same period Exxon stock rose 20 percent. And the S&P 500 Index more than doubled.

BP's failure to show that it cared can be seen in stark contrast with the way another leader dealt with a potentially devastating scandal involving his organization.

Showing You Care: Australian Defence Force

The Australian Army, formally known as the Australian Defence Force, or ADF, is a small but proud fighting force. And it is a faithful ally of the United States, fighting beside American troops in all wars for the past century. It has been in continuous operations in Afghanistan for 15 years.

In June 2013, the ADF discovered that a group of soldiers, who called themselves the "Jedi Council," had formed a sex ring that took surreptitious pictures and videos of women with whom their members were having sex, and then shared the images and videos among themselves. At the same time the ADF was struggling with the harassment of female solders by male soldiers, and bullying of seemingly weaker soldiers by stronger ones.

When this broke, the chief of the army, Lieutenant General David Morrison, spoke directly to the Australian army by video. He began by naming the problem:

> [The alleged] conduct, if proven, has not only brought the army into disrepute, but has let down every one of you and all of those whose past service has won the respect of our nation. Evidence collected to date has identified a group within our ranks who have allegedly produced highly inappropriate material demeaning women, and distributed it across the internet and Defence's email networks. If this is true, then the actions of these members are in direct contravention to every value the Australian Army stands for.[73]

He then stated the ADF's values and expectations for those who serve:

> I have stated categorically many times that the Army needs to be an inclusive organization in which every soldier, man and woman, is able to reach their full potential and is encouraged to do so. Those who think that it is okay to behave in a way that demeans or exploits their colleagues have no place in this army...

> On all operations female soldiers and officers have proven themselves worthy of the best traditions of the Australian Army. They are vital to us maintaining our capability now and into the future.[74]

He then challenged those who believed such behavior was acceptable:

> If that does not suit you, then get out. You may find another employer where your attitude and behavior is acceptable, but I doubt it. The same goes for those who think that toughness is built on humiliating others.

> Every one of us is responsible for the culture and reputation of our army, and the environment in which we work.

> If you become aware of any individual degrading another, then show moral courage and take a stand against it.[75]

He closed by declaring his commitment:

> I will be ruthless in ridding the army of people who cannot live up to its values, and I need every one of you to support me in achieving this. The standard you walk past is the standard you accept.

> If we are a great national institution – if we care about the legacy left to us by those who have served before us, if we care about the legacy we leave to those who, in turn, will protect and secure Australia – then it is up to us to make a difference. If

you're not up to it, find something else to do with your life. There is no place for you amongst this band of brothers and sisters.[76]

Whenever I show the video to students or clients, whether military or civilian, I get a consistent response. They conclude that General Morrison truly cares for the well-being of the troops under his command, both male and female. And they conclude that he is an outstanding leader.

In the year after the video, the ADF and law enforcement conducted investigations and legal and administrative proceedings. More than 170 ADF personnel were disciplined, including ten soldiers who were fired.[77] After he retired from the ADF, General Morrison was named 2016 Australian of the Year, for his commitment to gender equality, diversity, and inclusion.[78]

Key Takeaways from This Chapter

Crisis management is the management of choices at a turning point where an organization's destiny can go one way or another. Organizations that get through crises well make smart choices at the right time.

But there is often a kind of agony in the decision-making process. The key to getting the decision right is to think clearly. And thinking clearly means using the right decision criteria – the right basis for choice.

Using the right criteria allows a leader and organization to make smart choices in a matter of minutes.

But most leaders apply the wrong criteria because they ask the wrong questions. They ask some version of *What should we do?* or *What should we say?*

The challenge with this kind of question is that it focuses on the **we** – on the entity or leader in question – rather than on what really matters. This leads to saying things that make the leader feel good but that predictably alienate stakeholders. We saw such examples in the cases of both Netflix and BP.

What is needed is a different kind of thinking that begins not with **I/me/we/us** but with **they/them**. And that's because of the way trust works.

One common goal in a crisis is to maintain or enhance the trust of those who matter – shareholders, employees, customers, regulators, etc.

And trust arises when stakeholders' legitimate expectations are met. Trust falls when expectations are unmet.

Because trust is the consequence of fulfilled expectations, the right question to ask when determining the best course of action in a crisis is not *What should we say?* or *What should we do?*

Rather, think of the stakeholders who matter to your organization. Then, with those stakeholders in mind, ask:

What would reasonable people appropriately expect a responsible organization or leader to do when facing this kind of situation.

Asking this question is the most important concept in this book; the most important element of mental readiness.

Framing decisions in light of stakeholder expectations leads to smarter choices faster, and maintains stakeholder trust.

For any stakeholder group we can answer this question to a very granular level:

> ➤ To the level of a large universe, such as all employees, or to a small universe, such as only those unionized hourly workers on the second shift of a particular factory.

> ➤ To the level of all regulators or of particular regulators of a single regulatory agency.

> ➤ To the level of all customers or to only those customers who bought a certain product at a certain retailer on a certain day.

There are many ways to identify such expectations. To start, if there are legal or regulatory requirements, reasonable people would appropriately expect a responsible organization or leader to meet those requirements.

Similarly, does the company have a statement of values, a brand promise, or a code of ethics? Reasonable people would appropriately expect a responsible organization to fulfill the promises that it has set, either explicitly or implicitly.

But regardless of the particular expectations, there is a common expectation that applies to all stakeholder groups all the time: In a crisis, all stakeholders expect a responsible leader or organization to care.

To care that something has happened; to care that people need help; to care that something needs to be done.

The single biggest predictor of loss of trust and confidence is the perception that an organization or leader does not care.

So effective crisis response begins with a timely demonstration of caring. And it continues with a persistent demonstration that the organization and its leader continue to care, for as long as the expectation of caring exists.

What it takes to show we care may vary across time, across stakeholder groups, and across forms of crisis. But that we need to show we care does not change.

Showing we care is not sentimental. It is a leadership discipline; part of mental readiness to do what is necessary to protect trust and confidence in a crisis.

Chapter 4:
Decision Criterion #2: When to Do It?

The decision criterion for **what to do** is the answer to the question *What would reasonable people appropriately expect a responsible company or leader to do in this situation?* And whatever other specific expectations may exist, the common expectation among all stakeholder groups is that the company or leader cares.

But when should an organization in crisis show it cares? The common debate is whether to let people know about a negative event before it has already become public, or to wait until the news of the crisis is already out there. Indeed, most leaders are reluctant to disclose bad news first because they hope they can continue to contain or reverse the crisis.

Just as in considering **what to do**, there is a rigor to considering **when to do it**. That rigor begins with understanding the patterns of what works and doesn't work, and why.

The First-Mover Advantage

The first pattern is this: There is a first-mover advantage in crisis response, just as there is in other elements of business.

The first-mover advantage shows that whoever is the first to define three things typically controls the interpretation of an event:

> ➤ The nature of the crisis itself.

> ➤ The organization's motives.

> ➤ The organization's actions.

If the organization itself effectively defines the nature of the crisis, its own motives, and the nature of its actions, the result is that it will likely demonstrate that it cares, and will deprive critics and others of the opportunity to portray the organization as uncaring.

But if the organization does not take the first mover advantage, others can define it in unflattering ways.

Crisis guru Jim Lukaszewski notes,

> Every hesitation, marginal or confused response will energize victims, survivors, critics, public authorities, folks with their own agendas, and increasingly trigger social media activity.[79]

In the BP case described in the Chapter 3, BP lost the first mover advantage and therefore it allowed its critics, adversaries, the media, and social media to define the crisis: *BP was building an unsafe rig that blew up.* They also defined BP's motives: *Tony Hayward – and therefore BP as a whole – doesn't care about people or the environment, but only about himself and BP.* And they also defined the company's actions: *BP doesn't know what it's doing.*

Indeed, the former *Wall Street Journal* reputation beat reporter, Ron Alsop, in his book *The 18 Immutable Laws of Corporate Reputation*, describes the likely result of others defining a crisis, motives, and actions:

> Flailing around and looking helpless aren't inspiring to your stakeholders.[80]

And Tony Hayward certainly came across as flailing around and helpless, but not at all sympathetic.

Sometimes, as in the BP case, silence is a reflection of lack of readiness. Sometimes, though, it is intentional.

A significant challenge to showing care quickly is that all too often well-intended lawyers will counsel an organization to do or say little or nothing in the early phases of a crisis. Usually the lawyers are motivated by a desire to protect the company from increasing the risks in any future litigation about the crisis. But an undue attention to future litigation risk can cause serious and immediate strategic and operational harm to the organization. So just as every crisis is a business problem before it is a communication problem, every crisis is a business problem before it is a legal problem.

And a big part of the business problem is this: Loss of stakeholder trust is likely to have a profoundly negative effect on a company's competitive position. In fact silence is at the core of most subsequent reputational harm and loss of trust, according to crisis guru Jim Lukaszewski. He says,

> Silence is the most toxic strategy an organization or leader can choose. It is toxic to reputation, toxic to leadership, toxic to internal communication; toxic to an organization's legacy and toxic to any reasonable future explanation of what occurred.[81]

Not only is silence toxic, according to Lukaszewski, the explanation for being silent is almost always unconvincing.

> For honorable companies, products, and individuals there is no reasonable, sensible, believable, credible, or convincing explanation for why there was no communication, even for a brief time.[82]

Lukaszewski reports that he and other crisis advisors have clients who:

...have executed sophisticated, well-thought-out, credible, and near-perfect response activities and plans. But because they failed to speak immediately, even in the face of reasonably brief delays of an hour or two, all their work in preparation gets characterized as stumbling, fumbling, mumbling, and bungling. No amount of after-action analysis can credibly walk the response scenario back to explain why silence occurred.[83]

As covered in the last chapter, trust is the consequence of expectations fulfilled. Trust is maintained or rises when expectations are met; trust falls when expectations are not met.

There are three reasons silence in the early phase of a crisis becoming public can be so toxic:

> When stakeholders expect an organization to care, silence is interpreted as indifference – as the absence of caring. And as a result, trust falls. Or worse, silence can also be further interpreted as a tacit affirmation of guilt ("They must be guilty: why else would they refuse to say anything?"). And in the silence, stakeholders tend to interpret the organization's crisis as an integrity lapse, even as the organization may understand the crisis to be a routine operational setback.

> Worse, silence invites the media, social media, critics, and adversaries to seize the first mover advantage and to paint the organization as uncaring. So the nature of the crisis gets exaggerated negatively; the company's motives are characterized as unethical or lacking in integrity; and the company's actions are characterized as too little, too late, or self-protective.

> Even worse, if silence continues when there is an expectation of caring, then victims, critics, adversaries, the media, social media, politicians, and opportunists can begin to rally public opinion against the organization. This is when we see calls for boycotts, protests, pickets, petitions, and also calls for investigations, lawsuits, and for leaders to be fired. And when the late-night comedians weigh in, things get even worse.

Ronald Alsop, in *The 18 Immutable Laws of Corporate Reputation*, notes that:

> Crises aren't like fine wines; they don't improve with age. A communications void is highly dangerous during a time of crisis. Silence gives critics time to gain the upper hand and reinforces the public's suspicion that a company must be guilty. Without information from the company, rumors and misinformation can proliferate fast.[84]

So how can an organization find the balance between keeping trust and protecting itself in any future litigation? The key is to identify the categories of things that can be disclosed without unnecessarily acknowledging blame, guilt, or liability. In general, even risk-averse counsel, when pressed, will agree that the following, in whole or in part and properly drafted, would not necessarily increase risks in future litigation:

> Acknowledgment: A statement of awareness that something has happened.

➢ Empathy: If there are or may be victims, an expression of empathy or sympathy.

➢ Values: A declaration of the organization's values, such as "our first concern is the safety of our employees…"

➢ Approach: A summary of the kinds of actions taken or to be taken, such as "we are working with first responders and public safety officials, and will continue to do so until all employees are accounted for."

➢ Commitment: Setting future expectations, such as "we will continue to monitor the situation and will provide a public update when we know more."

Once counsel agree to those categories, which can happen in advance of a crisis, it is possible to draft a core standby that can be issued before news of the situation is otherwise public.

In our experience, a stand-by statement with those categories is sufficient to secure the first-mover advantage and demonstrate that the organization cares, without triggering undue legal liability.

Those same categories can also be the outline for a substantive statement, either when exercising the first-mover advantage, or later. Indeed, in the case of the Australian Army sex ring scandal, Lieutenant General Morrison followed just those categories:

➢ Acknowledgment:

Evidence collected to date has identified a group within our ranks who have allegedly produced highly inappropriate material demeaning women, and distributed it across the internet and Defence's email networks.

➢ <u>Empathy</u>:

[The alleged] conduct, if proven, has not only brought the army into disrepute, but has let down every one of you and all of those whose past service has won the respect of our nation. If this is true, then the actions of these members are in direct contravention to every value the Australian Army stands   for.

➢ <u>Values</u>:

I have stated categorically many times that the Army needs to be an inclusive organization in which every soldier, man and woman, is able to reach their full potential and is encouraged to do so. On all operations female soldiers and officers have proven themselves worthy of the best traditions of the Australian Army. They are vital to us maintaining our capability now and into the future. Those who think that it is okay to behave in a way that demeans or exploits their colleagues have no place in this army.

➢ <u>Approach</u>:

If that does not suit you, then get out. You may find another employer where your attitude and behavior is acceptable, but I doubt it. The same goes for those who think that toughness is built on humiliating others. Every one of us is responsible for the culture and reputation of our army, and the environment in which we work. If you become aware of any individual degrading another, then show moral courage and take a stand against it.

➢ <u>Commitment</u>:

I will be ruthless in ridding the army of people who cannot live up to its values, and I need every one of you to support me in achieving this. The standard you walk past is the standard you accept. If we are a great national institution – if we care about the legacy left to us by those who have served before us, if we care about the legacy we leave to those who, in turn, will protect and secure Australia – then it is up to us to make a difference. If you're not up to it, find something else to do with your life. There is no place for you amongst this band of brothers and sisters.[85]

The Golden Hour of Crisis Response

Of course, the best way to control the communication agenda is through the first mover advantage: Be the first to fully define the crisis, your motive, and your actions. And thereby show you care before others can define you as uncaring.

But what if that's not possible? If something happens unexpectedly? Or if others start talking about you before you're ready? Then there's a need to be nimble.

In fact, very often an organization cannot get the first mover advantage. That's because some unexpected event will happen and become public before the organization can mobilize a public demonstration of caring.

In these circumstances, it's important to understand the Golden Hour of Crisis Response.

The Golden Hour doesn't refer to a specific number of minutes, but rather to the observation that incremental delays in showing that an organization cares can lead to greater-than-incremental harm.

The idea of the Golden Hour arose out of emergency medicine. For example, the longer it takes to get competent medical care after a serious accident or heart attack, the slimmer the chances of survival. Medical procedures that would work in the first few minutes would be woefully inadequate 90 minutes later. That's because the patient's condition is dynamic – it is constantly changing. It isn't enough to address the patient's condition at the moment of injury. Rather, medical professionals know that they need to address the medical condition at the moment of treatment. And the longer it takes to get the treatment, the more robust the response will have to be.

The same applies in the quest to maintain trust in a crisis. The longer it takes to show we care, the harder it becomes. That's because more and more people are reaching conclusions about the situation, making judgments, and believing and acting on what they hear. What would have been sufficient in the early phases of a situation becoming public would be woefully inadequate hours or days or weeks later.

It is much harder to restore trust that has been lost than to preserve it in the first place. And companies get a much higher return on investment of time, energy, and treasure when they maintain trust rather than try to restore trust. So the longer it takes to show we care, the more we are at risk of losing trust.

But just because a bad thing has happened and become public doesn't mean that trust has already been lost. It takes some time for word to spread, and stakeholders don't appropriately expect a responsible company to be public with a response in the moment of crisis. So they give organizations a small benefit of the doubt for a limited amount of time. And if a company can show it cares within that window, trust can be maintained.

The general principle in applying the Golden Hour in a crisis is the rule of 45 minutes, six hours, three days, two weeks. That's the sequence of disproportionate effects that arise in particular intervals in the cycle of visibility—what used to be called the "news cycle" but with the ubiquity of social media is now far more widespread. This principle suggests that it's possible to show we care, but that the longer it takes to organize a sufficiently persuasive response, the harder it becomes.

The Golden Hour of Crisis Response

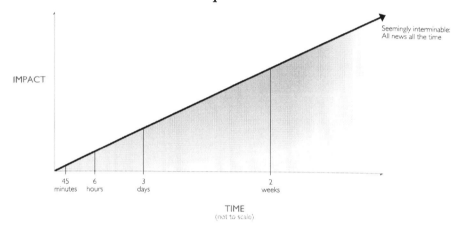

[Illustration by Adam Tiouririne]

Here speed is important – speed defined not as impulse but as the predisposition to make sound decisions quickly and to communicate them effectively.

If an organization can effectively show it cares within the first 45 minutes of an event, incident, or issue becoming public from some external source, relatively few stakeholders will have heard of the issue from others, and things are likely to settle down with minimal loss of trust, and likely no long-term harm. Very often a stand-by statement with the categories noted above is enough to show care quickly, even after initially losing the first mover advantage.

But if an organization misses the first 45 minutes, given the proliferation of social networking and citizen journalism, the likelihood is that more and more people will very quickly hear about the issue, with critics, adversaries, commentators, and others defining the nature of the crisis, the organization's motives, and its actions.

It is still possible to take control of the communication back, but it will be harder: the organization will need to reach more people, and overcome more competition for attention. And some people may have already formed opinions that will be very hard to change, including losing trust in the organization. But if it can demonstrate caring within the first six hours of the issue becoming public, then things should settle down relatively quickly.

As in the first-mover advantage and in the first 45 minutes, a well-crafted standby statement may be sufficient to show care in the first six hours. But stakeholder expectations may require providing more detail about the actions taken so far than a similar statement in the first 45 minutes.

If it takes more than six hours for an organization to define the crisis, its motives, and its actions, then it will be at risk for three days. That's because of the dynamics of daily newspaper publication and television news broadcasts, along with television and social media reaction to the initial story or stories, and any second-day newspaper stories and subsequent reaction. During this period, many more people are being made aware of the issue by critics, the media, or others. And the company and its leaders are more and more at risk.

It is typically within this window that victims, opportunists, activists, critics, and media begin to call for boycotts, petitions, firings, investigations, and lawsuits. But if within three days the organization can show it cares, the situation should resolve itself. But what it takes to show it cares is much more difficult on the third day than in the first 45 minutes or six hours.

If it takes more than several days for a company or its leaders to define to show caring, then significantly more people will know about the crisis, and it will be even harder to resolve it. And because of the publication schedule of weekly magazines, weekly newspaper sections, weekly blogs, and weekly television programs, the likelihood is that a controversy will be alive for at least two weeks.

If it takes more than two weeks to define the crisis, motives, and actions, then there's a very good chance of significant damage, sometimes irreparable. We saw that with Tony Hayward and BP: He became untenable as CEO and had to leave the company.

Decision Criterion for When: The Four-Question Test

Just as with the decision criteria for **what to do**, the criteria for deciding **when to do it** are based on stakeholders' expectations and their likely reactions. And as with the criteria for **What**, the key is to ask the right questions. We have found that four questions in particular are most productive. A Yes answer to any one of them is sufficient to give an organization and its leadership confidence that engaging stakeholders is a wise move.

We advise our clients to use these four questions as the explicit decision criteria in their crisis plans, and to get agreement in advance from all relevant parties involved with approval in crisis – the lawyers, business, heads, PR head, etc. – to use these questions to determine when to engage stakeholders.

The four questions are these:

1. **Will those who matter to us expect us to do or say something now?**

   If so, we should do and say what stakeholders expect. We should not do or say things that violate expectations, such as when BP CEO Tony Hayward said that the Gulf of Mexico was very large and the amount of oil being released was tiny in relation to it. Rather, we should do and say things that show we care.

   If the answer is Yes, there is no need to move on the other three questions. But if the answer is No, then we should move to the second question.

2. **Will silence be seen by our stakeholders as indifference or as an affirmation of guilt?**

If so, then we should engage stakeholders in a way that shows caring. But if the answer is No, we should consider the third question.

3. **Are others talking about us now, thereby shaping the perception of us among those who matter to us; is there reason to believe they will be soon?**

This is an effective way to address whether to engage when we are the subject of social media visibility. Just because someone tweets about us doesn't mean we should engage. But if the tweeting is likely to be noticed – either directly or through other media – by those who matter to us, then we should engage before those who matter to us have heard from others. If the answer is No, we should move to the fourth question.

4. **If we wait do we lose the ability to determine the outcome?**

Just because something isn't yet public is not necessarily a reason to use the first mover advantage. But if we are at risk of losing the first mover advantage, we should engage before we have lost it. This is often the case when a rumor is circulating; when documents have been leaked; in litigation when we know our adversary will be filing potentially inflammatory documents in court. In such instances using the first mover advantage allows us to shape our stakeholders' interpretation of the events before our adversaries have contaminated our stakeholders' understanding of us.

If the answer to all four questions is No, then we have an opportunity to monitor and to prepare, to rehearse, to draft documents, to secure approvals, and otherwise get ready to engage. Then, when the answer to any one of the questions becomes Yes, we can engage effectively. And we'll have either the first mover advantage or we will respond sufficiently quickly within the Golden Hour that there will be minimal loss of trust.

United Airlines: Mishandling the Golden Hour

We can see the power of the disproportionate impact of a small delay in showing care in the example of a defining crisis affecting United Airlines.

On the evening of Sunday, April 9th, 2017, passengers had boarded a United Express flight from Chicago's O'Hare International Airport to Louisville, Kentucky. United Express is a commuter arm of United Airlines and an integral part of the United Airlines system. That particular flight was operated by Republic Airline under the United Airlines brand.

Soon after the flight boarded, four United Express crew members arrived at the gate, hoping to secure seats to Louisville, from which they were scheduled to fly the next day. They had been booked on an earlier flight that had not taken off because of mechanical issues.

The airline faced a choice. It needed the flight crew to get to Louisville that night to prevent cancellation of the next day's flight. But 100 percent of the seats on the plane were already taken and all the passengers were already on board. The airline then followed a standard procedure. It made an announcement about the need to free four seats, and offered passengers $400 plus a hotel room and meals if they would give up their seat and fly to Louisville the next day. None of the passengers took the offer. The airline doubled the payment, but again, no one took the offer.

Federal procedures and United Airlines' own Contract of Carriage called for compensation of up to $1,350 for giving up a seat, but the airline did not offer that amount. After the passengers declined the $800 offer, the airline announced that four people would be randomly chosen to give up their seats. It then announced the four names. Two of the four passengers disembarked. But a third and fourth refused. David Dao, a 69-year-old doctor who was an immigrant from Vietnam, and his wife, Teresa, refused to get off the plane, saying he needed to see patients the next morning.

When it became clear that Dr. and Mrs. Dao would not get off the plane, the airline called Chicago Aviation Authority security officers. Three security officers boarded the plane. Dr. Dao told them that he was a doctor who needed to see patients the next day, and that he would not get off the plane.

One of the security officers then grabbed Dr. Dao, who screamed in pain, and the officers lifted him from his seat and forcibly laid him down in the aisle. In the process, Dr. Dao's face hit the armrest of a neighboring seat, causing a concussion, breaking his nose, and breaking two teeth. An officer then dragged Dr. Dao by his arms backwards toward the front of the plane. The other passengers yelled in shock at the officers.

Some time after being ejected from the plane, a bleeding and clearly disoriented Dr. Dao rushed back onto the plane, and paced around the back of the plane reciting over and over, "I have to go home. I have to go home…"

Dr. Dao was again removed from the plane, and it eventually took off for Louisville.

Overnight the video of Dr. Dao screaming and being dragged down the aisle went viral on Twitter and Facebook, and soon was trending throughout social media. It was the subject of extensive press coverage the next day.

At 12:30 the next afternoon, about 18 hours after the incident, United Airlines published a tweet on its official Twitter page. Under the title "United CEO response to United Express Flight 3411," the tweet read, in its entirety:

> This is an upsetting event to all of us here at United. I apologize for having to re-accommodate these customers. Our team is moving with a sense of urgency to work with authorities and conduct our own detailed review of what

happened. We are also reaching out to this passenger to talk directly to him and further address and resolve this situation. – Oscar Munoz, CEO, United Airlines.[86]

Although the statement itself was timely, the content and tone were all wrong. To begin, the first sentence seemed to suggest that it was United Airlines that was having a difficult time. But the second sentence captured public attention. The apology for "having to…" suggests that what the CEO was sorry for was the need to move passengers, rather than for the treatment of those passengers, especially Dr. Dao. But the next words were even more inflammatory. What was he apologizing for? Having to "re-accommodate" the passengers. The word re-accommodate seemed to be a euphemism; a benign thing. Reaction was fast and fierce. A passenger named Maryrose Bisagna tweeted a response:

> I'm a frequent flier of yours. This morning I chose to "reaccommodate" thousands of $ in biz to @SouthWestAir. #bummer.[87]

The United statement went viral on both social media and mainstream media. Late night comedian Jimmy Kimmel opened his show that night with five minutes on the United controversy. He showed the audience United's CEO's tweet, and then said,

> That is such sanitized, say nothing, take no responsibility, corporate BS speak. I don't know how the guy who sent that tweet didn't vomit when he typed it out, but it's crazy.[88]

That initial tweet defined United's response. And it failed to show that United cared about what happened to its passengers.

Later that same day, a letter from CEO Oscar Munoz to all United employees was leaked and went viral as well. The text of the letter also seemed not to capture the gravity of the customer experience. That letter, in full, read:

> Like you, I was upset to see and hear about what happened last night aboard United Express Flight 3411 headed from Chicago to Louisville. While the facts and circumstances are still evolving, especially with respect to why this customer defied Chicago Aviation Security Officers the way he did, to give you a clearer picture of what transpired, I've included below a recap from the preliminary reports filed by our employees.
>
> As you will read, this situation was unfortunately compounded when one of the passengers we politely asked to deplane refused and it became necessary to contact Chicago Aviation Security Officers to help. Our employees followed established procedures for dealing with situations like this. While I deeply regret this situation arose, I also emphatically stand behind all of you, and I want to commend you for continuing to go above and beyond to ensure we fly right.
>
> I do, however, believe there are lessons we can learn from this experience, and we are taking a close look at the circumstances surrounding this incident. Treating our customers and each other with respect and dignity is at the core of who we are, and we must always remember this no matter how challenging the situation.[89]

Like the tweet, this letter is all framed in the context of United Airlines. It said that the passenger "defied Chicago Aviation Security Officers." Following the letter was a bulleted list of events, including this description of Dr. Dao:

> He was approached a few more times after that in order to gain his compliance to come off the aircraft, and each time he

refused and became more and more disruptive and belligerent.[90]

Soon after this letter became public, a passenger who had been sitting near Dr. Dao posted video of the moments before Dr. Dao was removed. In it, Dr. Dao is speaking calmly with security officers, acting in neither a disruptive nor belligerent manner.

The letter contributed to the impression that United did not care about its passengers, but only about itself and its employees. It seemed to be blaming the victim for what had happened to him.

These two communications, the original tweet and the employee letter, each under the signature of the United CEO, became the defining elements of United's point of view. Given that they were made well into the Golden Hour framework, they needed to be powerful enough to overcome the very negative visibility of the prior 18 hours. But they only made matters worse. Neither seemed to show that the airline cared; about Dr. Dao, the other passengers, or about the criticism it had been receiving.

The next day, Day 3, United tweeted a link to a statement labelled, "Statement from United Airlines CEO, Oscar Munoz, on United Express flight 3411."

The statement, in full, read:

The truly horrific event that occurred on this flight has elicited many responses from all of us: outrage, anger, disappointment. I share all of those sentiments, and one above all: my deepest apologies for what happened. Like you, I continue to be disturbed by what happened on this flight and I deeply apologize to the customer forcibly removed and to all the customers aboard. No one should ever be mistreated this way.

I want you to know that we take full responsibility and we will work to make it right.

It's never too late to do the right thing. I have committed to our customers and our employees that we are going to fix what's broken so this never happens again. This will include a thorough review of crew movement, our policies for incentivizing volunteers in these situations, how we handle oversold situations and an examination of how we partner with airport authorities and local law enforcement. We'll communicate the results of our review by April 30th.

I promise you we will do better.[91]

This time, in both tone and content, Munoz got it right. He described the event as horrific. He expressed empathy for Dr. Dao and the other passengers. He apologized. He declared that no one should be so mistreated. He committed to changing procedures to assure that such a thing would not happen again. In other words, he showed that he cared.

But it was too late. United had already been defined as uncaring. And it had been the lead story on the news and the top trending topic on social media for nearly 48 hours. And it had become the punchline of jokes by late-night comedians.

By the time the effective statement was issued, it was seen to be insincere and far too late. It wasn't enough to overcome the perception that United didn't care.

That night Munoz was live on ABC's *Nightline*. In the interview, which was rebroadcast the next morning on ABC's *Good Morning*

America, reporter Rebecca Jarvis noted that the incident had sparked outrage around the world and that there were numerous calls to boycott United. Jarvis asked Munoz how he felt when he saw the video of his passenger being dragged off of one of his planes. His response,

> It's not so much what I thought; it's what I felt. The word ashamed comes to mind. As I think about our business and our people, the first thing I think is important to say is to apologize to Dr. Dao, his family, the passengers on that flight, our customers, our employees. That is not who our family at United is. You saw us in a bad moment and this will never happen again on a United Airlines flight. That's my premise and that's my promise.[92]

The reporter asked why he did not communicate that shame, and noted that in his original statement he had apologized for "reaccommodating" the passengers, and how in his internal note to employees he had spoken of a belligerent and disruptive passenger. She asked why it took until Tuesday to offer a more full-hearted apology. He replied,

> I think my first reaction to most issues is to get the facts and circumstances. My initial words fell short of truly expressing what we were feeling.[93]

Asked whether his current apology was too little, too late, he said,

> It is never too late, first of all, to do the right thing. And again, my initial reaction to the process was to get facts and circumstances, and my words failed.[94]

In the interview Munoz reviewed the steps United would take to assure that such an incident not occur again. This includes "a deep and thorough review of a lot of our policies." He noted that United would look very carefully at the use of law enforcement aboard an aircraft.

The reporter asked Munoz what went wrong in this incident. He replied,

> It was a system failure. We have not provided our front-line supervisors and managers and individuals with the proper tools, policies, procedures that allow them to use their common sense. They all have an incredible amount of common sense, and this issue could have been solved by that. That's on me. I have to fix that.[95]

The reporter recognized that under the law a passenger on a plane must get off the plane when ordered to by flight officials. She asked Munoz whether Dr. Dao was at fault in any way. After a short pause, Munoz said,

> No. He can't be. He was a paying passenger sitting on our seat in our aircraft and no-one should be treated that way. Period.[96]

The reporter closed by asking whether Munoz had considered resigning. He replied,

> No. I was hired to make United better, and we've been doing that, and that's what I will continue to do.[97]

All of Munoz' statements on Tuesday and Wednesday were consistent with what reasonable people would appropriately expect a responsible airline CEO to do following such an incident. He expressed remorse; he apologized; he took accountability for the combination of failures that led to the incident; he committed to thoroughly review policies, procedures, and training; he committed to not using law enforcement to remove a passenger who was not a safety threat. But it was too late. If he had expressed those thoughts and conveyed those commitments as the first statement from the airline, he would have shown that he cared. And however dramatic the video may be, they would have been balanced by his statement, made ultimately in his second statement, "I deeply apologize to the customer forcibly removed and to all the customers aboard. No one should ever be mistreated this way."

But his failure to show he cared in the first statement allowed the media, social media, critics, adversaries, and opportunists to paint the airline as uncaring. And even though on the third day he was able to show he cared, by then the impression of United as uncaring was part of the popular culture.

That weekend United's indifference became part of a Saturday Night Live sketch, in very poor taste, lampooning White House Press Secretary Sean Spicer's recent gaffe about the holocaust. Melissa McCarty, playing Spicer, said "I'm sensitive to the fact that [holocaust victims] were sent there on trains, but at least they didn't have to fly United."[98]

On April 21st, twelve days after the incident, and nine days after Munoz' ABC interview, United filed notice with the U.S. Securities and Exchange Commission that Munoz had initiated a change in the company's contract with him that would have allowed him to assume the title of Chairman of the Board in 2018. The filing said that Munoz had left "future determinations related to the Chairman position to the discretion of the Board."[99] In other words, Munoz gave up his future position as board chair.

In his initial letter to employees, Munoz promised a review of policies and procedures by April 30th. On April 27th, United published its *United Express Flight 3411 Review and Action Report*. It is a candid and thorough examination of the series of failures that led to the report. It concludes with a set of changes to United policies and procedures, including:

1. United will limit use of law enforcement to safety and security issues only...
2. United will not require customers already seated on the plane to give up their seats involuntarily unless safety or security is at risk...
3. United will increase customer compensation incentives for voluntary denied boarding up to $10,000...
4. United will establish a customer solutions team to provide agents with creative solutions...
5. United will ensure crews re booked onto a flight at least 60 minutes prior to departure...
6. United will provide agents with additional annual training...
7. United will create an automated system for soliciting volunteers to change travel plans...
8. United will reduce its amount of overbooking...
9. United will empower employees to resolve customer service issues in the moment...
10. United will eliminate the red tape on lost bags.[100]

These steps are extraordinary, and are likely to make recurrence of such an egregious customer service failure far less likely. And Munoz deserves credit for both his humility in acknowledging his and his company's failures and voluntarily giving up the chairman job, and his resolve to address the underlying problems. In his ABC interview he had defined the cause of the incident as a system failure, and only meaningful changes in the system would prevent such a recurrence. And only a CEO could make those changes happen. And indeed, these ten steps, if implemented well, should change the system in powerful, if expensive, ways.

But note that such steps would have been far less necessary if United had showed it cared in a timely and effective way. And note that the announcement of the changes received very little media or social media coverage. Most airline passengers, and most Americans in general, continue to view United through the lens of their initial missteps.

Responding Within the Golden Hour

Consider two examples of companies that responded effectively within the six-hour window on crises that might have taken much longer for companies that were less-prepared: J.C. Penney and McDonald's Corporation.

In each instance trust was on the line. And in each instance the crisis came upon the company suddenly and unexpectedly, but each responded in such a timely and effective way that it suffered no lasting damage to reputation, trust, sales, revenues, or other measures of competitive advantage.

In early September 2011, during the back-to-school sales cycle, retailer J. C. Penney offered a back-to-school T-shirt for girls. The shirt was adorned with a saying in whimsical typeface: "I'm too pretty to do homework so my brother has to do it for me."

Some customers found the shirt offensive. A young woman saw a Facebook posting about the shirt and decided to do something about it. Lauren Todd launched a petition on the social network site Change.org, which allows individuals to initiate petitions online. Change.org, in turn, promoted the petition through Twitter and to parenting blogs, asking people to post directly onto J. C. Penney's Facebook page. Within a few hours more than 1,600 people had signed the petition. Posts on Twitter, Facebook, and the company's own website expressed outrage, and many of those posting (who identified themselves as mothers of school-aged girls) threatened to stop shopping at J.C. Penney unless the company pulled the shirt from stores.

By the end of the day, J.C. Penney did just that: it pulled the shirt from its stores and apologized. It posted on its various sites, "We agree that the 'Too Pretty' T-shirt does not deliver an appropriate message, and we have immediately discontinued its sale."[101] Once stakeholders saw the retailer doing the responsible thing, the controversy abated and the company suffered no meaningful harm to its reputation. And it had a successful back-to-school selling season.

Consider also how McDonald's Corporation responded to the sudden death of its CEO on the most important day of its 2004 business year. More than 12,000 people who ran 30,000 restaurants in 119 countries were assembling in Orlando, Florida to hear from the chief executive officer about the company's new strategy.

James Cantalupo, 60, had been brought back from retirement to preside over a strategic repositioning of the company. McDonald's, once an icon of American business, had struggled in recent years as customers complained about service and cleanliness, and health activists criticized the company's food and marketing for contributing to the United States' obesity problem.

Cantalupo took the helm at the end of 2002 and launched a strategy to change the company. He overhauled the menu to include alternatives to fried foods and sugary drinks. He added grilled chicken, salads, and healthier drinks to the McDonald's menu. He also discontinued "supersize" portions.

When Cantalupo took over, the company's stock was just over $15 per share, and the company had reported its first quarterly loss since it had become a publicly traded company 38 years earlier. But in the next quarter, as the new strategy and menu were rolled out, same-store sales jumped nearly 5 percent, the largest sales increase in five years. Same-store sales continued to rise for 11 consecutive months. The company ended the year with a fourth-quarter profit of nearly $126 million, compared to a loss of $343 million in the year-earlier quarter. And in the year just before the Orlando meeting, the stock price of McDonald's doubled, closing at just under $30 in the last trading session before the meeting.

By late April 2004, the people who owned and operated McDonald's restaurants were assembling in Orlando for their every-other-year meeting with the company's leadership team. It was to be their first meeting presided over by Cantalupo, the first since the new strategy was launched. And as the meeting opened on Monday, April 19th, they were eager to hear a progress update from Cantalupo and his team.

But Cantalupo never took the stage. He had died overnight, apparently of a heart attack. Paramedics were called to Cantalupo's hotel just after 3 AM. He died in an ambulance on the way to the hospital, where he was pronounced dead at 4:53 AM. Sheriff's deputies reported finding heart medication in the hotel room. The medical examiner said that the death was "probably cardiac related."

McDonald's announced Cantalupo's passing in a press release at 8:07 AM.[102] The financial markets reacted quickly, with analysts warning investors to sell McDonald's stock. They noted that the company's new strategy was still being rolled out, and without a clear successor it was not certain whether the strategy would be continued.

Some pundits on financial television programs noted the irony of Cantalupo's apparent cause of death – heart attack – and the criticism McDonald's had received for promoting unhealthy eating.

The risks to McDonald's were significant. The convergence of thousands of the company's most important stakeholders in one place at the very moment the CEO died was an unusual circumstance to begin with. The passing of the architect of the new strategy also put the company at risk of strategic drift. Operators of the restaurants came to the meeting expecting both an update on the strategy so far and clear guidance about the game plan for the rest of the year.

But by the time the New York Stock Exchange opened at 9:30 AM, the McDonald's board of directors had already met. Several directors were already in Orlando for the meeting with restaurant operators. They convened a board meeting, with other directors attending via telephone conference call. By 9:30 that morning they had selected Cantalupo's successor, Chief Operating Officer Charlie Bell. They announced his appointment as CEO at 10:42 AM.[103]

Bell took the stage in Orlando, and after an appropriate acknowledgment of his predecessor's passing, delivered the presentation Cantalupo would have given. The McDonald's strategy was affirmed. The audience responded well. The company went on to have a very successful 2004. And Cantalupo's menu remains substantially in place today.

The speed with which McDonald's took action was uncharacteristic of many companies. But that speed allowed it to keep its most important stakeholders – the men and women who run its restaurants – focused on its strategy and committed to making the strategy work.

McDonald's was able to move quickly for a number of reasons, but primarily because of Cantalupo's wisdom in establishing a succession plan for himself with the board. Although he had expected to serve for several more years, he had already completed his succession process when he died, and his successor had already been provisionally approved by the board. When he died, the board was faced simply with the task of formally ratifying the work it had already done. The board met immediately on hearing the news, and announced the new CEO as promptly as possible after making its decision.

McDonald's received widespread praise for its ability to name and announce a new CEO so quickly. The *Wall Street Journal* said,

> The swift decision gave immediate reassurance to employees, franchisees and investors that the fast-food giant has a knowledgeable leader in place who can provide continuity and carry out the company's strategies. It may also shift any spotlight away from McDonald's high-cholesterol, fat-rich foods and prove a savvy public-relations move.[104]

It noted that most companies are unprepared to name a new CEO, and have at best only a plan for an interim leader, what the paper called a "bus-crash envelope" – an envelope to be opened in the event the CEO gets hit by a bus or otherwise dies suddenly.

Jack Welch, former General Electric CEO, told the *Wall Street Journal,*

> If there's someone capable who can take over permanently, it's best to name that person quickly. But boards who haven't groomed someone for the job yet shouldn't make a call for the sake of making a call.[105]

He noted that his own board would have been able to name a successor within an hour if he had been suddenly unable to serve.

McDonald's ability to move quickly was also noted by governance experts. Jay Lorsch, a professor at Harvard Business School, told the *Wall Street Journal,*

> The speed with which they've moved is exactly what you would expect to happen, but few companies are as prepared as McDonald's appears to have been for this calamity.[106]

And Jeffrey Sonnenfeld, an associate dean at Yale University School of Management, told the *Wall Street Journal*,

> The worst-case scenario planning of most companies is only a Band-Aid transitional solution, not a strategic solution. McDonald's directors, by immediately naming a battle-tested insider, showed the wisdom of having a succession plan in place.[107]

Six months after Bell succeeded Cantalupo, McDonald's again faced a succession challenge. Bell, seemingly in good health at the time of his appointment, was diagnosed with colorectal cancer two weeks later. By late November Bell handed the reins to his own successor, James Skinner, a 33-year veteran of the company. Skinner committed to continue Bell's and Cantalupo's strategy. The markets were heartened by that news. *The New York Times* declared in a headline: "Change at Helm, but a Steady Course at McDonald's."[108]

The McDonald's board recognized the importance of moving quickly to demonstrate steady leadership at the top, especially as the company was transforming its operations. It took the responsible steps to be able to reassure stakeholders in a moment of sudden concern. And it engaged stakeholders promptly: in the case of the Orlando meeting, telling the 12,000 owners and operators the news, and in the case of the second succession announcement, in a matter-of-fact manner when Bell's decision to step aside was made.

Tempo: Be Effective Quickly

Speed isn't just acting quickly. Impulsive communication – such as BP CEO Tony Hayward's "I want my life back" quote – is counterproductive. Rather, speed is best understood as tempo: the consistent ability to be effective in a timely way. As with McDonald's, it's about more than just talking. It's about acting effectively and engaging stakeholders promptly.

The consistent ability to act and engage stakeholders quickly and effectively creates a competitive advantage in the best of times. But it is in the worst of times that tempo matters most: it can prevent a negative event from becoming a tragedy, or worse. It is precisely in high-stakes situations that stakeholders, critics, and adversaries look for leadership in the form of effective engagement.

Crisis guru Jim Lukaszewski offers a strategy to implement within the first hour or two of a crisis. He calls it the Grand Crisis Response Strategy, which consists of five steps:

1. Stop the production of victims.
2. Manage the victim dimension.
3. Indicate internally immediately.
4. Notify the indirectly affected (regulators, partners, neighbors, the affected but largely uninjured).
5. Manage the self-appointed and self-annointed: media, social media, the bellyachers, bloviators, back bench gripers, anyone who opts into the conversation on their own.[109]

Lukaszewski notes that failure to activate these five steps will cause additional victims, questions, misunderstanding, and collateral damage, which the organization in crisis will then also have to deal with. He notes that all five steps can be talked about and tweeted immediately.

Key Takeaways From This Chapter

When should an organization in crisis show that it cares?

Just as in considering **what to do**, there is a rigor to considering **when to do it**.

There is a first-mover advantage in crisis response: whoever is the first to define three things typically controls stakeholders' interpretation of an event:

➢ The nature of the crisis itself.

➢ The organization's motives.

➢ The organization's actions.

If the organization does not take the first mover advantage, others can define it in unflattering ways.

Silence is often a reflection of lack of readiness. Sometimes it is deliberate. But silence is the most toxic approach an organization can employ.

There are three central problems with silence in the early phase of a crisis becoming public:

➢ When stakeholders expect an organization to care, silence is interpreted as indifference – as the absence of caring. And as a result, trust falls. And in the silence, stakeholders tend to interpret the organization's crisis as an integrity lapse, even as the organization may understand the crisis to be a routine operational setback.

➤ Worse, silence invites the media, social media, critics, and adversaries to seize the first mover advantage and to paint the organization as affirmatively uncaring. So the nature of the crisis gets exaggerated negatively; the company's motives are characterized as unethical or lacking in integrity; and the company's actions are characterized as too little, too late, or self-protective.

➤ Even worse, if silence continues when there is an expectation of caring, then victims, critics, adversaries, opportunists, the media, social media, and politicians can begin to rally public opinion against the organization. This is when we see calls for boycotts, protests, picketing, petitions, and also calls for investigations, for lawsuits, and for leaders to be fired.

Organizations can find the balance between keeping trust and protecting themselves in future litigation by identifying the categories of things that can be disclosed without acknowledging blame, guilt, or liability. In general, even risk-averse counsel, when pressed, will agree that the following, in whole or in part and properly drafted, would not necessarily increase risks in future litigation:

➤ Acknowledgment: A statement of awareness that something has happened.

> ➤ Empathy: If there are or may be victims, an expression of empathy or sympathy.

> ➤ Values: A declaration of the organization's values, such as "our first concern is the safety of our employees…"

> ➤ Approach: A summary of the kinds of actions taken or to be taken, such as "we are working with first responders and public safety officials, and will continue to do so until all employees are accounted for."

> ➤ Commitment: Setting future expectations, such as "we will continue to monitor the situation and will provide a public update when we know more."

In our experience, a stand-by statement with those categories is sufficient to secure the first-mover advantage and demonstrate that the organization cares, without triggering undue legal liability.

Of course, the best way to control the communication agenda is through the first mover advantage: Be the first to fully define the crisis, your motive, and your actions.

But what if that's not possible? If something happens unexpectedly? Or if others start talking about you before you're ready? Then there's a need to be nimble.

In these circumstances, it's important to understand the Golden Hour of Crisis Response.

The Golden Hour refers to the observation that incremental delays in controlling the communication agenda lead to greater-than-incremental harm. The longer it takes to show we care, the harder it becomes. We saw this in the example of United Airlines.

What might have been sufficient in the early phases of a situation becoming public would be woefully inadequate hours or days or weeks later.

As United Airlines learned, it is much harder to restore trust that has been lost than to preserve it in the first place.

The general principle in applying the Golden Hour in a crisis is the rule of 45 minutes, six hours, three days, two weeks. This principle suggests that it's possible to show we care, but that the longer it takes to organize a sufficiently persuasive response, the harder it becomes.

If an organization can effectively define the nature of the crisis, its motives, and its actions within the first 45 minutes of an issue becoming public from some external source, relatively few stakeholders will have heard of the issue from others, and things are likely to settle down with minimal harm to trust and likely no long-term harm. Very often a stand-by statement with the categories noted above is enough to show care quickly, even after losing the first mover advantage.

But if an organization misses the first 45 minutes, more and more people will hear about the issue, with critics, adversaries, commentators, and others defining the crisis, the organization's motives, and its actions. It is still possible to take control of the communication back, but it will be harder: the organization will need to reach more people, and overcome more competition for attention. As in the first-mover advantage and in the first 45 minutes, a well-crafted standby statement may be sufficient to show care in the first six hours. But stakeholder expectations may require that the organization provide more detail about the actions taken so far.

If it takes more than several hours to define the crisis, motives, and actions, then a company and its leaders will be at risk for three days. During this period, even more people are being made aware of the issue by critics, the media, or others. And the company and its leaders are more and more at risk. It is typically within this window that victims, opportunists, activists, critics, and media begin to call for boycotts, petitions, firings, investigations, and lawsuits. But if within three days the organization can show it cares, the situation should resolve itself. But what it takes to show it cares is much more difficult on the third day than in the first 45 minutes or six hours.

If it takes more than several days for a company or its leaders to define the crisis, its motives, and its actions, then significantly more people will know about the crisis, and it will be even harder to resolve it.

If it takes more than two weeks to define the issue, motives, and actions, then there's a very good chance of significant damage, sometimes irreparable. We saw that with Tony Hayward and BP: He became untenable as CEO and had to leave the company.

Just as with the decision criteria for **What**, the criteria for deciding **When** to show care are based on stakeholders' expectations and their likely reactions. And as with the criteria for What, the key is to ask the right questions. We have found that four questions in particular are most productive. A Yes answer to any one of them is sufficient to give an organization and its leadership confidence that engaging stakeholders is a wise move.

The four questions are these:

1. Will those who matter to us expect us to do or say something now?

2. Will silence be seen by our stakeholders as indifference or as an affirmation of guilt?

3. Are others talking about us now, thereby shaping the perception of us among those who matter to us; is there reason to believe they will be soon?

4. If we wait do we lose the ability to determine the outcome?

If the answer to all four questions is No, then we have an opportunity to monitor and to prepare, to rehearse, to draft documents, to secure approvals, and otherwise get ready to engage. Then, when the answer to any one of the questions becomes Yes, we can engage effectively. And we'll have either the first mover advantage or respond sufficiently quickly within the Golden Hour that there will be minimal loss of trust.

Chapter 5:

Consequences of Lack of Mental Readiness:

10 Common Crisis Missteps

In Chapter 1, I noted that deep knowledge allows leaders to learn tough lessons without living those lessons directly. They do this by, among other things, studying the predictable patterns that play out in crises, including the patterns of missteps.

In the late 1980s I began noticing a pattern in crisis missteps that companies and organizations commonly make, and have kept an inventory of them ever since. At the Logos Institute for Crisis Management and Executive Leadership, we continue to maintain and build upon that inventory.

What is remarkable is that the pattern of missteps has not changed over the 30 years that I have been actively working on crises, even as technology, social media, and social norms have changed. And even through waves of corporate and economic failures, from the Enron/Anderson/WorldCom crises of the early 2000s. And even through terrorist attacks, through prolonged wars, through the emergence of cyber-attacks and hacking, through the financial meltdown of 2008, and through emergence of social media technology that obliterates the distinction between private and public behavior.

I have witnessed these missteps in organizations operating in North America, Europe, Africa, Asia, Australia, and South America.

They serve as a kind of common denominator in institutional responses to negative events.[110]

Some companies engage in each of these one at a time, and end up in deep trouble. Others engage in several simultaneously. While this can be quite painful, it at least has the virtue of speed.

What these missteps have in common is that they betray a lack of mental readiness; a failure to exhibit emotional discipline, deep knowledge, or intellectual rigor.

Enlightened institutions and their advisors are on guard against these behaviors, and act promptly to overcome them if they arise.

Anyone in a position to help handle crisis response, whether from within an organization or as an outside advisor, should be alert to signs of any of these behaviors.

The ten counterproductive behaviors are:

1. Ignore the problem
2. Deny the severity of the problem
3. Compartmentalize the problem
4. Tell misleading half-truths
5. Lie
6. Tell only part of the story; let the story dribble out
7. Assign blame
8. Over-confess
9. Panic and paralysis
10. Shoot the messenger

Here are the typical ways such counterproductive behaviors play out:

Misstep #1: Ignore the problem.

In Chapter 1, I quoted former General Electric CEO Jack Welch, who identified denial as a common pattern in crises. And he noted that dispensing with denial quickly is a key to effective crisis response. But it is remarkable how many organizations are unable to address crises directly.

Ignoring the problem takes a number of forms. One common form is simply a failure to recognize that a given event or issue is likely to become a problem. Instead, management keeps blithely on its path while the problem continues to fester. Whether the problem is staff disaffection, a restless employee who may become a whistleblower, a troublesome agitator out to provoke a fight with management, or internal control issues, the organization turns a blind eye and is then surprised when things blow up.

National Highway Traffic Safety Administration/Ford-Firestone

Take, for example, a defining crisis of the early 2000s, the significant safety issue affecting Ford Explorer cars equipped with Firestone tires. In 2000 the U.S. National Highway Traffic Safety Administration (NHTSA) ordered a recall of all Ford Explorer vehicles after a number of suspicious accidents in which the cars rolled over. Initially, NHTSA was praised for protecting consumers from unsafe cars. But during congressional testimony it became clear that NHTSA had known about problems with Firestone tires on Ford Explorers nearly 18 months before being prompted to act.

Initially cast as a hero, NHTSA suddenly came under sharp attack for its apparent indifference to the fact that lives were at risk. And because many fatalities had occurred during the time NHTSA knew about the problems, some senators blamed the agency for not preventing those deaths and serious injuries. *Time* magazine wrote,

> Last week testy legislators pilloried Susan Bailey, head of the National Highway Traffic Safety Administration, over the agency's slow-leak performance in the Firestone case.[111]

NHTSA's apparent indifference caused significant reputational harm to the agency and to its chief.

While the NHTSA case is in some ways extreme – lives were at stake – it can be instructive for less dramatic circumstances as well. One reason it is important for crisis advisors to be in the room when business decisions are made is because it is important to weigh the impact of decisions, including the decision to do nothing, on stakeholders. And to inventory those stakeholders' expectations.

The regular presence of a trained crisis advisor in management meetings can often subject seeming routine decisions to a test that otherwise wouldn't be made: what could be the impact of our doing nothing about this problem in trust, confidence, reputation, and our competitive position? Would doing nothing be seen as not caring, or as demonstration of guilt?

Sometimes, as in the NHTSA case, the problem is acute and presents itself dramatically. Sometimes it creeps up. One such example of ignoring a chronic problem is the case of the once storied accounting and consulting firm Arthur Andersen.

Arthur Andersen

For decades the gold standard of trusted accountancy, Arthur Andersen went out of business in 2002, just six months after it emerged as inextricably linked to the fraud scandal involving the energy company Enron.

But a close look at the firm in the years before the scandal shows that the Enron entanglements were a symptom of a much larger problem.

Barbara Ley Toffler, formerly a professor of ethics at the Harvard Business School, ran Arthur Andersen's Ethics & Responsible Business Practices consulting group. After the firm's demise in 2002, she became a professor at Columbia University's Business School and wrote a book diagnosing the root causes of the firm's collapse. She writes that:

> Arthur Andersen was a great and venerable American brand that had, over the course of the twentieth century, become a global symbol of strength and solidity. In my years working at Arthur Andersen, I came to believe that the white-shoed accounting firm known for its legions of trained, loyal, honest professionals – a place that once had the respect, envy, and admiration of everyone in Corporate America – had lost its way. The accountants and the consultants forgot what it meant to be accountable. The fall of Arthur Andersen, I believe, was no murder. It was a suicide, set in motion long before there was ever an indictment. Yet while the guilty verdict sealed Andersen's fate, by the time it came it was merely a formality, the last nail in a coffin whose grave had been primed for burial.[112]

Toffler says that her attempts to bring problems to management's attention were rebuffed. She says that it was clear to her – and to anyone who chose to see – that Andersen's culture had shifted powerfully to a short-term focus on profitability at the expense of its core values of independence and client service, what she termed "billing our brains out," regardless of the value delivered to the client, of unethical entanglements, or of suspect behavior.

Toffler describes a culture where every employee who had or might have anything to do with a client had to figure out a way to sell more services to clients, regardless of the client's need:

> Some would call this client service – but in my experience it seemed to be more about raping the client than serving it.[113]

Toffler's business was advising clients on ethical business practice, not serving as an in-house ethics officer for her own firm. But internal ethical issues came to her attention, including a partner who she says had taken his daughter and a client's daughter to a New York Yankees game in a limousine, which waited for the entire game, and then took them home. The partner directed that the expenses for the trip be billed to the client as an audit-related expense. She recounts,

> I could find no indication that ethics was ever talked about in any broad way at Arthur Andersen. When I brought up the subject of internal ethics, I was looked at as if I had teleported in from another world... The end result was the continual reinforcement of the idea that it was okay to play with numbers...The laxity of this approach would come back to haunt the firm later: Billing Our Brains Out or compromising quality was what we all had to do to get ahead – or to keep up.[114]

According to Toffler,

There was simply too much similarity of thought, too much acceptance that the way thing were done was the best simply *'because that's the way we do it'* to see that this culture was turning on itself.[115]

She concludes:

I believe strongly that the suicide of Arthur Andersen – and the assault on the investing public's trust – could have been avoided had people paid attention to the danger signs flashing everywhere in the late 1990s.[116]

Roman Catholic Priest Child Abuse

A far more painful example of ignoring the problem is the case of child sexual abuse by priests of the Roman Catholic Church. This was a wide-ranging crisis over many decades that came to light dramatically in 2002.

Let's begin where the crisis first broke: the Archdiocese of Boston, whose Archbishop was Cardinal Bernard Law, a powerhouse in both Boston society and Catholic Church circles.

The *Boston Globe* first broke the news that dozens of priests had sexually abused children, and that the Archdiocese had turned a blind eye to it for nearly 40 years. Although Cardinal Law was not implicated in the abuse, he was implicated in the absence of an appropriate response. There were suggestions that he knowingly assigned problem priests to different parishes, only to have the same problems recur. He was even said to have sent some of the most egregious offenders to other dioceses without warning the bishops there, even giving the suspect priests glowing recommendations.

The Boston Archdiocese initially sought to play down the significance of the accusations, defending Cardinal Law and other diocesan officials. More and more adults came forward to volunteer that they too had been abused as children, and groups of survivors began meeting to offer comfort and support. Priests who had not been implicated in abuse began to call for the Archdiocese to take significant steps, such as meeting with the victims or offering an apology.

The *Boston Globe*'s original story appeared in January, 2002. After nearly a year of media feeding frenzy, serial accusations, public protests, and litigation, Cardinal Law finally agreed to meet with the survivors in December. In a sermon during Mass he offered to meet with survivors, and also offered his first apology. But by then it was too late. Eleven months had passed during which the Cardinal and the Church were seen to be indifferent to the harm caused by the priests and by the Archdiocese's inaction upon learning of the problem.

With the Archdiocese on the brink of bankruptcy, Cardinal Law resigned that week. Note that Cardinal Law himself had not been accused of abusing any children. Rather, he was seen to be indifferent to the harm caused by priests in his archdiocese, and his departure was inevitable.

Cardinal Law left the United States and settled in Rome. In 2004 Pope John Paul II named Cardinal Law the Archpriest of the Basilica of Santa Maria Maggiori, a major papal basilica. He served in that capacity until 2011. As of 2017 he is the Cardinal Priest of Santa Susana, a parish that largely serves Americans in Rome.

After the Boston Globe broke the story about abuse of children, the Massachusetts Attorney General, Tom Reilly, launched an investigation in March, 2002, and in July, 2003 issued a comprehensive report. He found that:

> ...at least 789 victims between 1940 and the present filed complaints with the Archdiocese about sexual abuse. The investigation documented allegations of sexual abuse of children against at least 237 priests and 13 other Archdiocese workers. Of these 250 accused priests and Archdiocese workers, 202 allegedly abused children between 1940 and 1984. The remaining 48 people allegedly abused children during Cardinal Law's tenure as Archbishop.[117]

But as troubling as the Boston problems may have been, they were only a small part of a nationwide crisis involving sexual abuse of children by priests, and the inaction on the part of the National Conference of Catholic Bishops, the Catholic Church's governing arm in the United States. It was clear that the Church knew of the problem, which had been the subject of considerable press coverage and books in the late 1980s and early 1990s.

According to the *Boston Globe*, which won a Pulitzer Prize for its reporting of the sexual abuse scandal in the Church, eight U.S. bishops resigned between 1990 and 2002 for involvement in sexual abuse, seven involving children.[118]

More troubling, the Church itself was aware of the magnitude of the problem as early as 1985. Father Thomas Doyle was at the time a canon lawyer and official in the Apostolic Delegation, essentially the Vatican's embassy in Washington, DC.

He and two colleagues, one a priest and the other a lawyer, responding to an onslaught of allegations in the early 1980s of child sexual abuse by priests, conducted an investigation and made a series of recommendations. Many of Father Doyle's recommendations are consistent with the best practices described in this book, essentially a model of what reasonable people would appropriately expect a responsible religious organization to do when it discovers priests abusing children.

The report included procedures for disciplining abusive priests, for notifying law enforcement personnel, and for protecting children from abuse. According to Father Doyle, copies of the report were sent to all U.S. bishops, and Boston's Cardinal Law acknowledged receiving a draft of the report.[119]

The report named the problem in very clear terms, even if it underestimated the eventual size of the problem:

> It is not hyperbolic to state that the dramatic description of the actual case contained hereinabove is indicative that a real, present danger exists. That other cases exist and are arising with increased frequency is evidenced by reports of same. If one could accurately predict, with actuarial soundness, that our exposure to similar claims (i.e. one offender and fifteen or so claimants) over the next ten years could be restricted and limited to the occurrence of one hundred such cases against the Church, ...then an estimate of the total projected losses for the decade could be established with a limit of one billion dollars.[120]

The report concludes (after 80 pages of considerable detail about the problem and extensive recommendations of potential solutions):

> Though each case of felonious sexual misconduct is bound to be different with regard to circumstances, notoriety, possibly liability, there is also a set of common threads which weave through all such cases. The very fact that these cases involve clerics of the Roman Catholic Church who have committed acts which are considered by society to be despicable and heinous and which have received a very high degree of publicity

in the media of late...make it imperative that there be comprehensive planning and specialized strategies for handling all such occurrences among the clergy. There is simply too much at stake for the Church, its leaders, its clergy, and its faithful not to attempt to provide the best possible response to the overall crisis."[121]

The report outlined a comprehensive approach to both dealing with problem priests (including their removal from the presence of children) and for preventing such problems from happening, ranging from the way priests are educated to how they are supervised and disciplined.

The report was distributed in 1985 to each diocesan bishop in the United States. According to Father Doyle,

> There was no response from anyone to this gesture. Some bishops, when asked by the press, indicated that they had found it helpful. The NCCB [National Conference of Catholic Bishops], however, never acknowledged its existence nor have they ever contacted [the authors] in relation to any of the meetings which they have had concerning the issue since that time.[122]

The Church took no meaningful steps to address the problems raised in Father Doyle's report. And note that Father Doyle's report named the problem in unequivocal terms, and outlined the predictable consequences of inaction and of action.

Only in the wake the Boston revelations in 2002, 17 years later, did the Church begin to take serious steps to address the problems, even convening a meeting of all U.S. bishops to develop guidelines. Critics challenge whether the reforms go far enough, noting, for example, that the reforms do not take a zero tolerance stance.

The harm caused by the Church's ignoring the problem is staggering. First, the reputation of the Catholic Church, and of other religious denominations, suffered significantly. The Church's moral authority was seriously challenged. Many parishes reported significant declines in contributions, church attendance, and membership. Individual priests reported in the aftermath that they feared they were no longer trusted by parishioners.

Although the numbers are difficult to confirm because so many settlements are bound by confidentiality, the cost of all the legal settlements and litigation was estimated in 2003 to be more than $1 billion. The Boston Archdiocese, strapped for cash, had to sell its real estate and other assets to remain solvent, even selling the Archbishop's residence for about $100 million, and slashed social service programs.[123]

But the far greater cost was the toll on the hundreds, potentially thousands of children who were hurt by priests between 1985, when the Church was formally put on notice that it had a problem, and 2002, when it was finally moved to take action.

The moral authority of the clergy on matters completely unrelated to the scandal also suffered. An editorial at the time in a publication of Americans for Religious Liberty noted,

> The fallout from the clergy sex abuse scandal, the cover-ups, and denial of responsibility by the bishops ...have deepened the crisis for America's 62 million-member Catholic Community ... The moral authority of the U.S. hierarchy has been so weakened and compromised that major statements adopted by the bishops on national policy are now ignored and/or ridiculed. A case in point is the bishops' denunciation of a potential U.S. invasion of Iraq by a 218-14 vote margin.

The bishops warned that the Bush administration's plans violate the historic principles of a just war ...The national press ignored what should have been regarded as a significant statement. Conservative commentators linked the bishops' cover-up of priestly crimes to their political statements. Said the usually pro-Catholic *National Review*, 'U.S. Catholic bishops, unable to discipline priestly molesters and the bishops who protected them, have turned their attention to Iraq. Once again, the shepherds fail their flock.'[124]

The tragedy is that the problem was so preventable. If only the Church, or the Boston Archdiocese, had named the problem clearly: not that they were at risk of embarrassment or of legal exposure, but that their priests were violating their fundamental responsibility to protect the weak; that they had committed crimes. Indeed, this is the language in Father Doyle's report.

If only they had taken the pain and in 1985 disciplined the priests, apologized to the families of the affected children, paid restitution in legal settlements, established a zero tolerance policy, and then enforced it. These actions were recommended in Father Doyle's report, but the Church ignored it. Such moves would have been painful. But they would have been far less painful, far less harmful to the reputation of the Church and its leaders than the pain the Church ultimately suffered.

And more important, such moves could have prevented the abuse that later took place.

A good contrast to the Boston Archdiocese's handling of the problem is the way the Archdiocese of Santa Fe, NM handled similar issues. According to a page one *USA Today* article,

"Beginning in the 1960s, New Mexico's parishes served as a national dumping ground for pedophile priests. After doing time in a rural rehab center geared toward alcoholics, they slipped into sunbaked, Hispanic hamlets and set about their unholy work. By the '90s, 187 lawsuits were filed against dozens of priests."[125]

In 1993 the Archbishop resigned following a CBS *60 Minutes* broadcast alleged that he had been sexually involved with three young women. The new Archbishop, Paul Shaheen, concluded that sexual abuse of any kind was unacceptable. He did what reasonable people would appropriately expect a responsible bishop to do when his diocese was facing such a serious problem of priest abuse of children.

Rather than ignore the problem, or hope that victims remained unidentified, he invited victims to come forward. He hired a private investigator to search for victims who had not yet been identified. He fired priests who had been implicated in abuse. He did not interfere with law enforcement's efforts to prosecute the priests, six of whom were eventually convicted of criminal charges. He met with the victims and apologized for the behavior of the priests. He met with the communities and disclosed the problems, apologized, and outlined the steps that were being taken to prevent similar issues, including a zero tolerance policy.

Before Archbishop Shaheen's arrival the Archdioceses' finances had been very weak, membership and attendance had declined, and new priests had been reluctant to move to Santa Fe because of the stigma attached to the Archdiocese. Within two years of Archbishop Shaheen's arrival membership had grown by 17,000, the finances recovered, and many new priests were thoroughly vetted and assigned to parishes.

Archbishop Shaheen told *USA Today*,

> The lessons we learned? Apologize, and take steps toward zero tolerance. The church will come through, but the temple must be cleansed.[126]

Archbishop Shaheen's handling of the problem in Santa Fe is in stark contrast to Cardinal Law's handling of it in Boston. Archbishop Shaheen named the problem and took the pain. He showed he cared. In other words, he did what reasonable people would appropriately expect a responsible church leader to do. Cardinal Law ignored the problem and was ultimately seen to be indifferent to the harm that had been caused.

The two cases illustrate a pattern noted earlier: that in a crisis, the nature and severity of the underlying event is not what determines reputational and operational harm, but rather the timeliness and effectiveness of the response. The nature and severity of the problems in both Boston and Santa Fe were very similar. But the timeliness and effectiveness of the response was significantly different, with dramatically different outcomes for the dioceses, the bishops, and the reputation of the Church in general.

To be sure, in the decade and a half since the Boston Globe broke the story, the Church has made slow but steady progress. Cardinal Law's successor as Archbishop, Cardinal Sean O'Malley, has become a leader in the broader Church move to protect children and to hold priests and their supervisors accountable. And he was instrumental in getting both Pope Benedict XVI and Pope Francis to meet with, apologize to, and commit to protect victims of priestly abuse. Cardinal O'Malley is also heading the Pontifical Commission for the Protection of Minors, the Vatican's effort to develop policies and procedures to protect children around the world from abuse by priests. The Commission, initiated by Pope Francis, has initiated training for church staff worldwide. It has also created a Vatican tribunal to judge cases of bishops who are accused of failing to protect children. As of the Summer of 2017, as this book is going to press, the tribunal has not yet met.

Cardinal O'Malley has moved the Church a long way since he took over the Boston Archdiocese in 2003. The tragedy is that it took so long for the Church to take the problem seriously.

Misstep #2: Deny the severity of the problem.

A somewhat more subtle behavior is to deny the severity of the problem.

Unlike ignoring a problem, the denial is grounded on recognition that something is wrong and needs to be addressed, but refusing, for whatever reason, to take the appropriate action now.

Usually the refusal is based on the understandable human tendency to try to avoid confrontation, unpleasantness, embarrassment, and difficult decisions. Sometimes the refusal is based on arrogance, sometimes on fear of short-term financial harm.

While understandable, such self-deception is a harmful response to adversity, for several reasons. First, it makes a candid assessment of the situation, and the choice of options based on reality, less likely. Second, the denial may entrench leaders into positions from which retreat may be politically difficult, preventing people from mobilizing quickly to solve the problem. Third, for as long as the problem is unresolved the company is at risk of having events careen out of its control. When it finally comes around to admitting that it has a problem, it may be too late to overcome the damage that has already taken place.

Salomon Brothers

One classic example of denying the severity of the problem is the discovery of improper trading in U.S. government bonds by the investment firm Salomon Brothers. (The firm had been my client in the mid-80s but by the 1990s no longer was.) In 1991 Salomon Brothers was a Wall Street powerhouse, best known for its dominance of the market for U.S. government bonds, but also a strong force in the stock market and in mergers & acquisitions.

The firm had been the subject of a 1990 book by Michael Lewis, *Liar's Poker*, which highlighted the firm's rough-and-tumble culture, where the highest praise was to be known as a "big, swinging dick."[127] The firm's Chairman, John Gutfreund was profiled in a *BusinessWeek* magazine cover story in the late 1980s as the "King of Wall Street."

In April 1991 Salomon Brothers discovered that one of its young traders had found a way to corner the market in U.S. government bonds. Such a maneuver, while potentially profitable, was also illegal. The firm called the trader before the compliance department and management, and gave him a slap on the wrist. It then sent him back to the trading floor. Significantly, it did not follow the procedures required by the two regulatory agencies that supervise the firm: the Federal Reserve, which regulates the market for U.S. government bonds; and the Securities and Exchange Commission, which regulates the U.S. securities markets. Salomon Brothers did not notify its regulators, and it did not take steps to assure that no further improper trading took place.

Not surprisingly, several months later the same trader was again cornering the market for U.S. government bonds. This time, though, the improper trading was discovered not by Salomon Brothers, but by a London asset management firm that traded with Salomon Brothers. The London firm notified U.S. regulators.

Those regulators descended upon Salomon Brothers and discovered not only that the London firm was correct that improper trading was taking place, but also that such improper trading had taken place in the Spring and that the firm had not followed the required procedures.

A story at the time in *BusinessWeek* magazine quoted incredulous Wall Street executives:

> One high official of a rival brokerage fervently believes top management is innocent of wrongdoing. "John Gutfreund and Salomon President Tom Strauss and Salomon Vice-Chairman John Meriwether had no idea what was going on," he asserts. "I would bet my life on it." Apparently, however, the three top Solly honchos weren't too anxious to do anything when they found out what was going on. The Aug. 14 statement says that Gutfreund, Strauss, and Meriwether were told of one of the unauthorized February bids in April but failed to report it to the government "due to lack of sufficient attention to the matter."[128]

The regulators required drastic action on the part of Salomon Brothers. Not only was the trader fired; several levels of management, including the Chairman, John Gutfreund, were also fired. The firm was vulnerable to collapse. At the last minute Warren Buffett was installed as Chairman, using his reputation for high ethical standards to keep the firm afloat.

In 1997 the firm was sold to Traveler's Insurance, which in 1998 merged with Citibank to become Citigroup. Salomon Brothers merged with Traveler' previous acquisition, Smith Barney, to form Salomon Smith Barney. Some years later the "Salomon" dropped out of the name. Within 10 years the franchise that had been known as the King of Wall Street had ceased to exist.

The tragedy of the Salomon Brothers example is that it was so preventable. Traders at the time expressed surprise at the act that would ultimately bring down the firm:

> One of the reasons for the disbelief expressed on the Street is the clumsiness of the machinations confessed by Salomon. "Just a silly thing to do," says Steve Modzelewski, a former Salomon trader. "Ethics aside, it's embarrassing to do something so simple-minded... if you were going to break the law, you could be more clever."[129]

If only Salomon Brothers had not shown, in their own words, "lack of sufficient attention to the matter." If only the firm had not seemed indifferent to the harm caused. If only the firm had taken the pain in April when it first discovered the improper trading in April, by genuinely disciplining the trader, notifying the regulators, and establishing procedures to prevent recurrence, it would not have been subject to such draconian penalties in August. And the chain of events that led to the firm's disappearance might have been avoided.

Misstep #3: Compartmentalize the problem.

A common reaction in large companies or in companies where fiefdoms or strong boundaries exist is to compartmentalize a problem.

While acknowledging that a problem exists, the company that compartmentalizes sees the problem as falling into a convenient administrative category: It's not our problem, it's a supplier's problem; it's not a product problem, it's a packaging problem; it's not a corporate problem, it's a field office problem.

But the outside world rarely sees the company in unrelated administrative categories: to the outside world, your problem is your problem, period.

Unlike ignoring a problem, compartmentalization has the virtue at least of acknowledging that a problem exists and taking steps to deal with it. But compartmentalization creates further difficulties. By insisting on a compartmentalized worldview, the company risks seeming defensive or disingenuous. And the compartmentalization sometimes means that the resources of the whole organization are not available to solve the problem, often with disastrous consequences. Some famous (more precisely, notorious) examples follow here.

Exxon Valdez

In 1989 the oil tanker Exxon Valdez struck some rocks on a reef off of Alaska's Prince William Sound, spilling 11 million gallons of crude oil. The Exxon Valdez oil spill became emblematic of mishandling a crisis, because of Exxon's seeming indifference to the harm that had been caused. But within Exxon, the company initially thought it was responding appropriately to the spill.

It had mobilized its transportation subsidiary, responsible for moving oil, and was implementing its transportation subsidiary crisis plan from the subsidiary's headquarters in Houston.

But the corporation as a whole was not active in the initial aftermath of the spill, having delegated to a responsible subsidiary.

Because Exxon defined the problem as a transportation subsidiary problem, it did not assign the full weight of the corporation to solve the problem. All the while, the media was broadcasting ghastly images of sea birds and mammals dying horrible deaths on the rocky beaches of Prince William Sound, and observers, government officials, and residents were loudly asking, "Where is Exxon?"

For more than a week Exxon seemed absent from the scene; seemed not to care. As public anger grew, Exxon remained puzzled by the response, believing that the problem was being taken care of.

About a week after the oil spill, protesters gathered in front of Exxon's headquarters in New York, and using scissors cut their Exxon credit cards on live television. Exxon executives were puzzled by the public reaction, since the credit cards were a product of the refining and marketing subsidiary, not of the transportation subsidiary.

Finally, after more than 10 days, Exxon mobilized its full corporate resources, and Exxon's Chairman finally went to Alaska to apologize for the spill and to commit Exxon's resources to fixing the problem. But it was too late. Despite significant work on Exxon's part, and the expenditure of billions of dollars, Exxon's reputation suffered significantly.

Contrast Exxon's compartmentalized view with the behavior of Johnson & Johnson during its crisis with Tylenol. Although Tylenol was marketed by Johnson & Johnson's McNeil Consumer & Specialty Pharmaceuticals subsidiary, when seven people died in 1982 after taking Tylenol tablets, Johnson & Johnson mobilized its full corporate resources, and did not delegate the solution to the problem to its subsidiary.

For decades Johnson & Johnson has been given credit for its handling of the Tylenol crisis, while Exxon, until BP took the mantle from Exxon, was seen as the emblem of ineffective crisis response for its handling of the Exxon Valdez spill.

And more than 35 years after the Tylenol crisis, Johnson & Johnson is still held in high regard. In 2003, Harris Interactive named Johnson & Johnson as having the best corporate reputation in America for the fourth straight year. And *Fortune* magazine named Johnson & Johnson as the sixth most admired company in America and the first among pharmaceutical companies. And both cited the 1982 Tylenol response as a key reason.[130]

Compartmentalizing a problem is failure to think clearly, a lack of intellectual rigor, that allows one's corporate perspective to govern the naming of and solution to the problem. Companies naturally want to contain damage as low in the organizational structure as possible, and to avoid over-reaction to any given problem. And there's certainly value in containing such damage where possible. But thinking in corporate silos or according to some organizational chart is an unproductive way to define the problem: certainly those who matter to the company are unlikely to so define the problem.

The criterion to determine whether to define the problem as a corporate problem or as a subsidiary problem is, like the other criteria in this book, based on stakeholder expectations. If customers, media, investors, regulators, and others define the problem as a corporate problem, then it is a corporate problem. If those who matter to you define a problem as a corporate problem, their expectations will center on a corporate response. And they will look to the company as a whole for a timely and robust response. Failure on the part of the corporation to respond quickly and adequately will be seen as not caring.

In Exxon's case, the company was further burdened by the name of the oil tanker, which shared a corporate name: Exxon Valdez. Perhaps if the company transporting the oil had been unrelated to Exxon, and if the tanker had been named generically, Exxon might have been given more of the benefit of the doubt. But since the first name of the tanker was Exxon, and since the transportation subsidiary was wholly owned by Exxon, the public saw the spill as the company's responsibility. To the public, Exxon was Exxon, period.

American Airlines

Another risk of compartmentalized thinking is failure to recognize that a problem even exists. Take, for example, the problem at AMR Corp., parent of American Airlines. Like many U.S. airlines, American was suffering in the wake of the 9/11 attacks and the economic downturn of the early 2000s. In April, 2003 the company's Chairman and CEO, Donald Carty, went from hero to ousted CEO within one week for failing to appreciate that compensation of his top management team is not unrelated to the compensation of union workers.

On April 16th, 2003, according to the *Chicago Tribune*, Carty struck a deal with several unions that would have helped protect the company from bankruptcy. The deal included significant concessions by three different unions. During his negotiations, Carty did not disclose to the unions that he had also arranged to pay bonuses to his senior management team and to protect their pensions in the event of a bankruptcy.

It is absolutely understandable how an executive could compartmentalize the two issues: Executive compensation is a matter for the board and leadership to determine, and is unrelated to the collective bargaining that a company undertakes with the union. But however rational such compartmentalization may be from the corporation's point of view, Carty's actions took place as executive compensation was becoming a national contentious issue, and as it was being framed as a zero-sum game. His deal with the unions was announced the same week that *Fortune* magazine ran its cover photograph of a CEO as a pig in a pinstriped suit to accompany its criticism of excessive executive pay.

The unions learned about the executive pensions three days after their own deal was announced – on the day the deal was ratified – from a regulatory filing. The unions felt betrayed by management, and asserted that the withholding of the information showed bad faith on management's part.

The *Chicago Tribune* reported:

Just last Wednesday, Carty emerged triumphant outside the company's Ft. Worth headquarters, having engineered an unlikely restructuring of his airline's labor deals. The three main unions narrowly agreed to wage cuts and work-rule changes worth $1.8 billion a year. Three days later, employees were calling for Carty's resignation. The same night the pact was approved, American disclosed in a regulatory filing that it planned to award retention bonuses to its top executives.

It also disclosed that it had taken steps to guard the pensions of 45 senior managers. The unions became outraged that executives withheld the information during the labor talks. The uproar forced the airline to drop the bonuses. But American said it would leave the pension trust in place. While executive perks are not illegal, management lost credibility with employees. "If someone has misled you to encourage you to take a personal loss, why would you believe his judgment later?" said Laura Hartman, professor of business ethics at DePaul University.[131]

Carty's resignation was announced five days later. Carty was the victim of an all too common institutionalization of thinking, where different functional areas – in this case, executive compensation and collective bargaining with unions – were seen in the minds of those who mattered to be intimately related. The compartmentalization that was an administrative convenience during normal times became a barrier to effective management of labor issues during financial distress and highly emotional negotiations with the union.

Bridgestone/Firestone

Another element of compartmentalization is compartmentalizing the solution.

For example, in 2000 Bridgestone/Firestone recalled its tires following a National Highway Traffic Safety Administration order and significant negative publicity. A large number of Ford Explorer vehicles had been involved in fatal accidents after the Firestone tires on the cars came apart. But Bridgestone/Firestone, the maker of Firestone tires, had a problem of capacity, and was unable to offer exchanges nationwide in a timely way.

Reasonable people would appropriately expect a responsible tire manufacturer to replace all the suspect tires quickly; and if there weren't enough tires available, to buy equivalent tires from other manufacturers.

But Bridgestone/Firestone chose a different path. Because the incidence of tire separation that led to fatalities seemed to be correlated to high temperatures, Bridgestone/Firestone initially established a timetable under which only tires in certain U.S. states – Texas, Florida, Arizona, and California – would be exchanged quickly.[132]

Consumers in all other states would have to wait, in some states up to a year or more. The announcement was made in August, when temperatures in Northern states were also high. Predictably, the prospect of waiting to fix a major safety problem outraged consumers, legislators, and regulators.

Bridgestone/Firestone dropped its plan and offered fast exchanges in all states.[133] But by then the reputational harm was done: Firestone was seen not to care, to be uninterested in its customers' safety and indifferent to the risks to customers.

If it had been interested in safety, the reasoning went, Bridgestone/Firestone would have offered a prompt recall to everyone, even if that meant that Firestone had to pay for the installation of competitors' tires. By the time it did make that offer, it had lost the trust and confidence of many consumers, and had squandered precious time when it could have been finding a more robust solution to the problem.

Compartmentalizing the solution is another example of unclear thinking. It was easy to predict the consequences of a rationed approach to replacement of tires: that it was untenable. But rather than begin with what reasonable people would appropriately expect a responsible company to do, and therefore how consumers, government officials, and the media were likely to respond to a rationed approach, the company began with reference to a capacity problem and asked customers to wait. Predictably, customers rejected the rationed approach, and the Firestone brand suffered yet further harm.

The New York Times

One final manifestation of compartmentalization is to compartmentalize the solution by mis-defining a company's role in the aftermath of a crisis. One example is the way *The New York Times* handled the early phases of its discovery in 2003 that one of its reporters, Jayson Blair, had invented stories and lifted material from other newspapers' stories.

On Sunday, May 11th, *The New York Times* shocked readers with a 7,000-plus word article about the Jayson Blair affair. The article was an impressive feat of journalism. It revealed what Blair had been found doing, and noted that a quick review of Blair's story by editors had found problems in 36 out of 37 stories in a narrow time period.

The story, which appeared prominently on the front page and on several inside pages, named the problem in the first paragraph:

> A staff reporter for *The New York Times* committed frequent acts of journalistic fraud while covering significant news events in recent months, an investigation by *Times* journalists has found. The widespread fabrication and plagiarism represent a profound betrayal of trust and a low point in the 152 year history of the newspaper. The reporter, Jayson Blair, 27, misled readers and *Times* colleagues with dispatches that purported to be from Maryland, Texas and other states, when often he was far away, in New York. He fabricated comments. He concocted scenes. He lifted material from other newspapers and wire services. He selected details from photographs to create the impression he had been somewhere or seen someone, when he had not. And he used these techniques to write falsely about emotionally charged moments in recent history, from the deadly sniper attacks in suburban Washington to the anguish of families grieving for loved ones killed in Iraq.[134]

The article quoted editors, the publisher, and others at the newspaper. And as a work of journalism, it was very compelling. But as a work of crisis communication it left much to be desired.

It left unanswered how such a situation could have been allowed to happen; whether the reporter was treated differently from other reporters because of his race (Blair is African-American); whether heads would roll in senior ranks for allowing it to happen; what steps would be taken to prevent a recurrence. It failed to address what reasonable people would appropriately expect a responsible newspaper to do when it had uncovered what the paper itself called frequent acts of journalistic fraud.

By allowing the crisis to unfold as a story – as a work of journalism – The New York Times Company and *The New York Times* newspaper missed an opportunity to control the way the Blair situation was communicated, and to announce steps it was taking to make matters right.

The key to the *Times'* approach, and to why it was inadequate as a crisis communication process, is embedded in the very first sentence of the story: "…an investigation by *Times* journalists has found."

By allowing the story to be told as a process of journalism, and as the fruits of a journalistic investigation, The New York Times Company and *The New York Times* newspaper allowed the bad news to be presented by a third party, even if it was a third party employed by the newspaper. And because the reporters working on the story did not have access to all of the facts, nor the ability to mandate actions, the leadership of the *Times* was called to account by its many stakeholders for a more complete explanation. And when the story appaered many other media reached out for comment or explanation, which was not forthcoming.

Key among the key stakeholders was the *Times* newsroom – the reporters and editors who work at the *Times*. They had an angry meeting with executive editor Howell Raines four days after the story appeared, during which they had heard little from their bosses.

Remarkably, the account of the meeting appeared in the *Times* the next day with the notation that because the meeting had been closed to news coverage, the reporter covering the story for the *Times* had been excluded from the meeting – even though it was an all-employee meeting and he was an employee. He relied, instead, on third-party accounts and on a tape recording made "by someone in the audience." The reporter wrote,

> The executive editor, Howell Raines, spent much of the time at the nearly two-hour meeting responding to often angry complaints and questions about his management style, according to people who attended the session...He said later, 'I was guilty of a failure of vigilance that, since I sit in this chair where the buck stops, I should have prevented.'[135]

Admitting to a failure of vigilance during a private meeting, even one attended by journalists, is not the same as publicly admitting to a failure of vigilance. Allowing the failure of vigilance to be reported by a third party, who was absent from the meeting, as the first public communication about that failure of vigilance, four days after the scandal became public, allowed the company to lose the first mover advantage – to define the nature of the crisis, the company's motives, and the company's actions. And Raines and the *Times* leadership seemed unprepared for the deluge of criticism that followed that admission.

Raines and Gerald Boyd, managing editor, resigned (upon being dismissed) on June 5th. *The Times* later instituted a number of changes in leadership and new structures to prevent a recurrence of the Blair problems.

Raines, who had been executive editor – the top person in the news organization – when the Blair scandal broke, finally told his side of the story one year later. In a 23-page article in the *Atlantic* monthly magazine, Raines describes his experience at the *Times* and his handling of the scandal.

Buried deep in the piece is a single paragraph that describes how he chose to handle the crisis. And his revelation is stunning. He says that he asked assistant managing editor Allan Siegal and two others to supervise a reporting team to research and write a story about the Blair deceptions. Raines writes:

> I urged them to work as fast as possible, but not to sacrifice accuracy for speed. I also told Al that he should put whatever they learned in the paper according to normal editorial standards and without showing the story to [managing editor] Gerald [Boyd] or me.[136]

In other words, the two senior-most managers of the newspaper were to have no idea what was to be published about the largest betrayal of trust in the history of the newspaper until the story appeared.

Raines confirms that he did not see the story until the day of its publication. In fact, he didn't exhibit any particular sense of urgency to read what it said. He was not in the newsroom – or even in New York – when the story was published. He was fishing with a friend on a drift boat on the Delaware River that Sunday morning. He writes, "I read the story in sections as the day unfolded, and I knew at that point that I was unlikely to survive."[137]

Raines and his boss, publisher Arthur Sulzberger Jr., abrogated their responsibilities as leaders by letting subordinates tell the story of what happened without the leaders themselves taking control.

Rather than do what reasonable people would appropriately expect responsible leaders of a journalistic organization to do – gather all the facts, determine corrective measures to take, and then disclose fully all they had discovered – they allowed middle-level editors and reporters to develop the sole formal communication about the scandal, and then let that news story in a single newspaper be the sole distribution channel for dissemination of news about the breach of the *Times'* standards.

To be sure, they did so from pure motives. For example, Raines writes that during a meeting before the story appeared, "someone used the term 'damage control.' I told the group that we were not in the damage control business. 'Full disclosure' would be our approach, I said."[138]

But paradoxically, full disclosure is not what happened. Rather, perhaps out of an aversion to "spin," Raines dismissed the significance of a non-business-as-usual approach, and instead, seduced by an idealized sense of the power of journalism, chose to let his journalists do the work of revealing their findings through, in his own words, "normal editorial standards." As a result, what was revealed was not full disclosure, but woefully incomplete disclosure and inadequate dissemination of what was disclosed.

It is also likely that Raines chose to recuse himself and managing editor Gerald Boyd from the process because they were likely to be criticized and he wanted to give his reporters license to pursue the investigation wherever it would lead them. This is an honorable impulse, but one that clearly backfired.

What was missing from Raines' prescription of the solution was a sense of options and of consequences. Raines did not think through (at least in his own retelling) alternative courses of action and the predictable intended and unintended consequences of each.

One predictable unintended consequence of not being shown the story before its publication, and of resisting anything that smelled of "damage control," is that Raines and his team were unprepared for the tough questions that were put to them, failed to address many of the predictable questions in the original communication, and continued to use processes of journalism – where the people writing the story did not have access to the newsmakers or to the content of their disclosures, except through third parties. They compounded their initial mistakes and made matters progressively worse, to the point that Raines' and Boyd's departure was a foregone conclusion.

One lesson here is that pure motives aren't sufficient to weather a crisis. Here Raines' pure motives led him to indulge his sense of honor in ways that predictably were inadequate to the challenge. And his dismissal was the direct result of that indulgence.

But the *Times* could have prevented much of the harm if it had not compartmentalized its identity – if it had not behaved first like reporters, and second like people invested with a public trust. Upon discovering the Blair deception, the *Times* assigned reporters to learn what they could and to report on it, without briefing management along the way.

A far more productive approach would have been for management to conduct the investigation (perhaps with outside help), to make the hard choices, and to disclose fully and publicly all it had learned, all it had decided, and what steps it was still expecting to take. And management could have disclosed their findings in ways beyond the pages of their newspaper. This kind of approach could have prevented piece-meal revelations and disclosure in private meetings four days after the initial story broke.

One challenge facing every organization in adversity is to be true to its own values while communicating effectively, fully, and consistently. But being true to one's values is not the same as practicing one's craft with a higher level of intensity. For example, reasonable people would not appropriately consider prayer to be an adequate response to a crisis involving clergy, nor litigation to be an adequate response to a crisis involving lawyers. Similarly, journalism was not an adequate response to a crisis involving journalism. Business as usual, even practiced to a high level of intensity and competence, will not work in a crisis.

Part of the problem may have been that the publisher of *The New York Times* newspaper was also the Chairman of The New York Times Company. By compartmentalizing his own role as publisher of the newspaper, his instinct called for journalism to be the solution to the problem. If he had thought instead as the chairman of a media company whose primary operating unit had a crisis, perhaps he could have directed a different kind of response, allowing the crisis to be communicated directly and in his voice rather than indirectly through the voice of reporters working for his newspaper.

Misstep #4: Tell misleading half-truths.

Another common misstep, usually driven by a desire to avoid short-term embarrassment, is to respond to a crisis by stringing together a series of statements that are each literally true, but that have the effect of misdirecting attention from the problem or of painting a false picture. While not exactly a lie – a deliberate untruth told with intent of deceiving – it is not quite the truth either. At best it is a half-truth. But the motive is usually to deceive, not to acknowledge or validate a concern.

This kind of behavior was practiced by the tobacco industry for years in response to questions about the link between cigarette smoking and cancer. The canned response by the industry was to say something along the lines of "there is no scientifically valid study that demonstrates that smoking causes cancer." For a long time this was literally true: it was impossible to point to an individual smoker and predict that he or she would contract cancer from smoking. But it was also irrelevant, because there was ample scientific evidence that smoking increased the risk of cancer, and that there was a non-trivial correlation between smoking and cancer.

A common way this misstep takes place is, for example, for a company that has an incident to neither acknowledge nor deny that the incident occurred but rather to say something that sounds definitive but that evades the question. This usually takes this form: Question: "Was there an emission of dangerous gasses from your factory?" Answer: "We remain in full compliance with all environmental regulatory standards."

If in fact there was an emission, it is far more constructive to acknowledge that an emission took place, describe what was emitted, describe whether that emission is cause for concern, and then to close with the statement that the company remains in compliance with all environmental regulatory standards (if that is true). One reason the half-truth is ineffective is that people have become conditioned to see it for what it is – a dishonest evasion – and to seek other evidence of the problem. Typically, the company eventually admits to the problem, but by then the company's credibility has been harmed. It looks like a company trying to hide an unpleasant reality. Worse, it has essentially challenged its adversaries to prove that it has a problem to begin with.

President Bill Clinton

We saw precisely this behavior from President Bill Clinton on the first days of the Monica Lewinsky scandal. On Wednesday, January 21st, 1998, an article appeared in the *Washington Post* reporting a rumor that the president may have had an affair with an intern. President Clinton was scheduled to appear on the PBS news program *NewsHour* with Jim Lehrer to discuss his State of the Union address, which was scheduled for the following week.

At the end of that interview Lehrer asked the president to respond to the Washington Post story. President Clinton used the present tense: "there is no sexual relationship."[139] Lehrer followed up, "So the reports in the Washington Post this morning were false?" The president replied simply that "there is no sexual relationship." This statement was literally true, because it was made in the present tense, and the sexual relationship, we now know, had been in the past.

But the answer was deliberately misleading because it painted a false picture, suggesting that the rumors of an improper sexual relationship with Lewinsky were false.

The predictable consequence of the half-truth was that political pundits and the president's adversaries, of which there were many, parsed his statement for days. There were continuous stories on network television about the president's precise words, and whether he was trying to get away with something. Reporters spent the rest of the week trying to get the president to address the past, even shouting above the roar of the president's helicopter while he was leaving the White House, "How about before? Did you <u>ever</u> have a sexual relationship before?"

Caught in the half-truth, President Clinton several days later told the whopper of a lie, asserting that he never had sexual relations with that woman, Lewinsky.

As President Clinton learned, a misleading half-truth, like the lie, is likely to be found out. Companies and leaders face the same consequences in being caught in the half-truth as in being caught in the lie: because they attempted to deceive, they lose credibility and are far less likely to be believed when they tell the truth.

The admonition against telling misleading half-truths doesn't suggest that a company shouldn't tell true statements that paint the company in a positive light. But the true statements a company tells should be grounded in a clear understanding of the reality of the situation, not on a deceptive foundation. They should attempt to elaborate on the acknowledgement of the problem, not to deceive.

Misstep #5: Lie about the problem.

One of the biggest mistakes that a company or leader can make is to lie about its problem.

As any ten-year old knows, the consequences of getting caught in a lie are more severe than the problem one lies about. As is often said, it's not the crime but the cover-up that causes lasting damage. For large organizations the harm to trust, reputation, and competitive position from getting caught in a lie can be greater and last longer than the underlying problem. In the case of public companies, lying about material events or a company's financial condition can subject a company and its management to SEC sanction or to prosecution.

Even in the case of private organizations, getting caught in a lie can diminish trust that can be difficult, and sometimes impossible, to restore. And the organization then suffers from doubt among its critical constituencies even when it is telling the truth.

Experience shows that the lie is often found out. And in an era where leaks are prevalent and private documents can easily become public, it is even more likely for disgruntled insiders to call attention to the lie.

Very often the lie is a panicked first response to the recognition that a problem exists, without recognizing that other people know the truth and have an interest in protecting themselves or in embarrassing the institution or its leaders.

In particular, a lie can be an invitation to one's adversaries, internal or external, to discover or to expose the truth. And when the lie is exposed, the company has a double burden: to solve the original problem that got it into trouble in the first place, and it has to do so in an environment where its credibility is diminished.

President Bill Clinton

Let's revisit President Clinton and the Monica Lewinsky scandal. After trying for several days to get away with the literally true statement intended to deceive, President Clinton told a lie about his relationship with Monica Lewinsky.

On Sunday, January 25th, 1998, he called the female members of his cabinet together for a previously-scheduled White House ceremony, and with them standing in the television picture with him, the President said, "I did not have sexual relations with that woman, Miss Lewinsky."

For the next eight months the presidency and the nation were diverted by the President's adversaries' attempt to catch him in the lie. Kenneth Starr, the special prosecutor investigating the President's affair, published an exhaustive report that contained the smoking gun: a dress owned by Lewinsky had the President's DNA on it. Confronted with evidence of his lie, President Clinton on August 17th, 1998 went before the nation in a televised address and admitted to his lie.

The House of Representatives, after extensive televised hearings, voted articles of impeachment. In early 1999 the Senate voted not to convict and remove the President.

But the President's legacy was forever changed. And his effectiveness as President was diminished.

As the President learned, once a leader or a company is seen to have lied about one problem, it will have great difficulty being believed in future crises. This is one of the many problems that plagued President Clinton. Soon after his apology for lying he ordered military action in the Balkans, citing a security threat. He was accused of engaging, in the phrase made popular by the movie of the same name, in *"Wag the Dog"* behavior, creating a military diversion to call attention away from unpleasantness.

Similar circumstances apply in the corporate sphere. I know of several companies that lied about their problems, got into trouble, and were unable to dig out; later, when the companies were being battered by rumors that were in fact false, they couldn't get anyone to believe them, and suffered unnecessarily.

Martha Stewart

Another striking account of the consequences of lying is the case of Martha Stewart, the founder and, at the time, the largest shareholder and chairman and chief executive officer of Martha Stewart Omnimedia. Among Stewart's personal investments were several thousand shares of ImClone, a pharmaceutical company founded by Stewart's friend, Sam Waksal. Both Stewart and Waksal used the same stockbroker, Peter Bacanovic of Merrill Lynch.

On December 26th, 2001,[140] Waksal learned that the U.S. Food and Drug Administration (FDA) had refused to review ImClone's promising cancer drug, Erbitux. On December 27th, Waksal and his family directed Bacanovic to sell their ImClone stock. Bacanovic, who was on vacation in Florida, directed his assistant to notify Stewart of the Wasksal's trade, an apparent violation of both Merrill Lynch rules and SEC regulations. The assistant left a message for Stewart, who was on vacation. Stewart later called the assistant, who conveyed Bacanovic's message, and Stewart directed Faneuil to sell her ImClone shares.

The next day, December 28th, ImClone announced the FDA decision, and the stock fell 18 percent. Soon afterward, the SEC began an insider trading investigation.

On January 7th, 2002 Bacanovic told the SEC that he and. Stewart had agreed on December 20th, that he should sell her ImClone shares if they ever fell to $60, which occurred on December 27th. On February 4th, Stewart told the SEC, federal prosecutors, and the FBI the same description of the agreement to sell if the stock fell to $60.

On June 12th, Waksal was charged with insider trading and Stewart issued a public statement describing her agreement with her broker to sell the stock at $60. One year later, in June 4th, 2003, Stewart and Bacanovic were indicted on several federal counts. Stewart resigned as chairman of Martha Stewart Omnimedia, but remained chief executive officer and a member of the board of directors. On June 10th, Waksal was sentenced to ten years in federal prison.

In 2004 Stewart and Bacanovic were tried in the U.S. Courthouse in Manhattan. The trial was a media circus that was widely covered on all major networks, including some who broadcast Stewart's arrival and departure each day. I counted 18 television broadcast trucks lined up in front of the courthouse one morning during the trial. Although the judge dismissed the sole securities fraud charge against Stewart, she let stand all other charges, which alleged that Stewart lied to investigators about the circumstances of her ImClone trade. On March 5th Stewart was found guilty of conspiracy, of two counts of making false statements, and of obstruction of justice. Bacanovic was found guilty of conspiracy, of making false statements, of perjury, and of obstruction of justice. He was found not guilty of making and using false documents.

Stewart resigned as a director and as chief creative officer of her company, having previously resigned as chief executive officer.

She served six months in a federal prison, and another six months of house arrest, and a further year of supervised release in which she needed court permission to travel beyond the southern part of New York State.

In the decade since she completed her sentence she has made a comeback, but she is no longer nearly as popular as before her downfall.

One interesting and tragic element of the entire Martha Stewart episode is that it was preventable. Apparently Stewart and her broker feared that their action could be seen by regulators to be insider trading. Rather than own up to their behavior, or even to defend it, their first resort was to lie: to invent a story justifying the trade for reasons other than knowledge of the Waksal trades.

According to testimony by Bacanovic's assistant at the trial, he left Stewart a message on December 27th, 2001 that ImClone stock was expected to trade down. She returned the call, and he told Stewart, per Bacanovic's direction, that the Waksals were selling their holdings. It is conceivable that she would have ordered the sale even in the absence of the knowledge about the Waksals, simply on the basis of the stock being expected to fall. Such discussions are commonplace among brokers and their customers.

But Stewart is herself a former stockbroker, who should have known that being told about the Waksals was improper, whether or not her sale of ImClone constituted insider trading. In fact, there was significant debate after her trade became known about whether such an act was insider trading.

In the end, Stewart was not charged with insider trading. Rather, she was charged with securities fraud, not for her trade but for her public statements about the order to sell if the stock fell to $60. The prosecutor's theory of the case was that Stewart had defrauded holders of her own company's securities, Martha Stewart Omnimedia, because of her lie. She was not charged in the ImClone sale itself. And in her trial the judge dismissed the securities fraud charge. So all the charges that the jury considered related to the lie she told investigators. In other words, she went to jail for the cover-up, not for the underlying crime, for which she was not convicted.

The day after Stewart was indicted, the *Wall Street Journal* editorialized about the foolishness of lying about a crime one has not committed: "Fibbing to investigators is always a bad idea: fibbing to them about why you were speeding when you really weren't speeding is an especially bad idea."[141]

Lying as a first resort (as Stewart was convicted of doing) or as a later resort (as President Clinton admitted doing) has predictable consequences that can be far more severe than the underlying offense. President Clinton was distracted from his official duties for nearly a full year and finished his second term much weaker than his first. Admission of his affair would have been painful but would probably not have resulted in impeachment. Stewart's reputation and wealth have both declined dramatically, but arguably less than they would have if she had confessed to an error in judgment and faced the consequences. In both cases the lies challenged their adversaries – President Clinton's political opponents and Stewart's regulators, prosecutors, and investigators – to find the evidence of the lies and to turn the evidence against those who had lied.

Misstep #6: Tell only part of the story, letting bad news dribble out over time.

Another common error many companies make, which is reflective of their failure to take the pain, is to admit only the least amount of information they can. This is almost always self-defeating because the bad news will almost certainly get out eventually. When companies are parsimonious with the bad news, reports of problems tend to dribble out over an extended period of time. The result is a stream of negative rumor, news reports, and gossip that keeps the company's troubles on people's minds.

The key principle for releasing information in a crisis is to bundle bad news within a single news cycle, and to unbundle good news over multiple news cycles. The bundling of bad news results in everything that would otherwise become known coming out all at once, preferably with a strong statement detailing what the company is doing about its problems. This generally pre-empts the desire of reporters and adversaries to show that the company has been less than forthright, and can expedite the process of recovering from reputational harm.

Another manifestation of dribbling bad news out is to withhold publicly available documents. This is counterproductive in several ways. First, the documents will get out anyway. Second, the attempt to withhold the documents paints the company as defensive and makes it look guilty. Third, the time and energy spent in trying to defend the withholding of documents could otherwise be productively spent dealing with the problem.

New York Stock Exchange

We saw just this behavior during the 2003 New York Stock Exchange compensation scandal. According to *The Wall Street Journal*, the New York Stock Exchange said it was withholding distribution of documents relating to Chairman Richard Grasso's compensation – documents totaling 1,200 pages – "in the interests of saving the world's forests." The claim provoked ridicule, because no reporters believed the restrictions were based on a genuine interest in preserving forests. In fact, two reporters from each news organization were permitted to examine the documents for two hours, and were permitted to take notes, but were not permitted to remove the documents or make copies.

The next day the Stock Exchange, realizing that its attempt to restrict access had backfired, changed course. *The Wall Street Journal* captured the absurdity of the exchange's environmental motive in the first paragraph of its story:

> So much for those trees. One day after the New York Stock Exchange said it would restrict distribution of 1,200 pages of documents relating to its chairman's contentious retirement package, 'in the interests of saving the world's forests," the

exchange decided to side with the logging industry. News organizations had been in a twitter all day because the Big Board refused to hand out copies of a pile of documents sent to the Securities and Exchange Commission...[142]

Even so, the exchange's change of heart was only half-hearted. According to *The Wall Street Journal*, "the media wouldn't be able to easily get a copy of the entire filing."[143]

Misstep #7: Assign blame, internally or externally, rather than fix problem.

A natural human tendency is to look for someone to blame when things go wrong. While understandable, assigning blame in the early phase of a crisis can be very counterproductive, for several reasons.

First, the media and industry gossips love conflict and clashes of personality. Assigning blame plays into these negative frame of references, and keeps the focus on things other than what the company is doing to solve its problems.

Second, time spent looking for and punishing a scapegoat could otherwise be better spent identifying the scope of the problem and taking steps to fix it. There will always be time to find and punish someone who is truly responsible for a problem. But the first task upon discovering a crisis should not be to find out who's at fault.

Bridgestone/Firestone and Ford Motor Company

Among the many missteps taken by Bridgestone/Firestone and The Ford Motor Company in the early phases of the crisis was the attempt by each to blame the other for the problem.

As news of the crisis broke in the summer of 2000, Bridgestone/Firestone blamed Ford for instructing its customers to inflate the tires to the wrong tire pressure; Ford blamed Bridgestone/Firestone for producing tires with a defect. All the while the public was less concerned with who was to blame than to be certain that it was safe to drive Ford Explorer cars with Firestone tires. Both companies lost the opportunity to demonstrate that their first concern was their customers' safety.

The one exception to the general rule against assigning blame is when the problem involves malfeasance or other clearly inappropriate behavior by an individual, who is clearly responsible for his or her actions. In this case dismissal or some other form of punishment is appropriately seen to be part of the solution, not a diversion from finding and fixing the problem.

The rule against assigning blame, rather, suggests that it is counterproductive as a first resort to try to deflect attention away from the company to some other entity.

Misstep #8: Over-react: "Confess" to more than actually happened.

One curious corporate behavior is to over-confess, or to over-react to a contained incident or event. While not as common as the behaviors noted above, over-confessing is common enough to warrant some discussion.

Over-confession tends to occur when the crisis prompts in the mind of management many other, unrelated frustrations, problems, or issues. The leader then is unable to draw a distinction between the present crisis and other everyday annoyances or unrelated problems, and proceeds to bare the company's soul about extraneous or petty issues that have no bearing on the crisis. The result can be focusing public attention on negative matters much broader than the crisis itself. More significant, the over-confession prevents leaders from focusing on the solution to the actual crisis, and can have a very negative impact on the morale of employees and on the confidence with which management is seen.

I had a client who engaged in just this behavior. Appearing on CNN to discuss a contained and low level crisis, the reporter asked how the CEO felt about the problem. The CEO took a deep breath, and unburdened himself of many frustrations, including his poor relations with his board, his inability to attract top talent to senior management positions, and declining market share, none of which were remotely related to the crisis. The reporter did not interrupt, but allowed the executive to continue rambling. The CEO did not last long in office. His self-indulgence, behaving in a public interview in ways more suited to a private therapy session, was his undoing. He was fired soon afterward.

Misstep #9: Panic.

Panic is a manifestation of lack of emotional discipline, and predictably leads to bad decision-making, unclear communication, distraction from one's business, or escalation of the crisis.

The panic can lead to a number of other problems. These can include paralysis, where people stop focusing on doing their jobs and where the company's work product (and potential revenues) grind to a halt. More commonly, panic leads to hastily-made and unproductive decisions that complicate or escalate the crisis. Panic can result in unclear internal and external communications, confusing people about what happened and what the company is doing about it. It can surface interpersonal or interdepartmental rivalries that get in the way of both good decisions and clear communication.

Another manifestation of panic is the desire of many people to become instant crisis managers, and to focus their time on dealing with the crisis. This is understandable, since a crisis can be a refreshing break from routine workflow, and can cause adrenaline to pump in those handling the crisis.

But too many people focusing on the crisis can cause two types of problems. On the one hand, there's the risk of a confused chain of command and of imprecise or overly complex tasking of crisis activities. On the other hand, every person who works on the crisis is not working on his or her regular job. If too many people are distracted for too long, a significant backlog of important work can arise, resulting in low productivity, impaired customer service, or worse.

For example, I know of a professional services firm that allowed all of its partners to participate in brainstorming the solution to a crisis over a period of months. A large number spent virtually all of their time doing so, arguing among themselves over the desired course of action. The result was predictable: almost nothing got accomplished

Helio Fred Garcia

to solve the crisis, since each partner proposed a solution that cancelled out another partner's proposed solution.

Worse, after several months without working for and billing clients, the firm became insolvent and had to sell itself to a bigger firm in order to meet its payroll and pay its bills. The desire to empower everyone to be a crisis manager cost the firm its independence. It isn't the crisis that brought down the firm: it's the firm's paralysis in the face of the crisis that did so.

This book is about mental readiness in a crisis. Another important element is operational readiness: having clarity of the processes by which a crisis will be managed. This includes designating a crisis team to focus on the crisis itself, while other leaders get back to the important work of leading the organization.

Misstep #10: Shoot the Messenger.

The final crisis misstep is the tendency of organizations to overtly or subtly punish people for bringing problems to management's attention.

Enlightened companies know that an open channel to report possible problems early, before they've grown to unmanageable size and complexity, is preferable to being unaware of a problem that could easily be addressed.

Companies whose cultures discourage the identification of problems typically find that problems are less likely to be reported up the chain of command. But that doesn't mean that the problems don't exist, just that they are being allowed to fester.

This predictably results in a company ignoring the problem, and can cast the company as indifferent to the harm it may be causing.

These ten behaviors are the common denominators of corporate and institutional dysfunction when things go wrong. They are manifestations of a desire to avoid facing hard realities. They result from inattention to consequences, and from allowing fear, anxiety, greed, or arrogance to govern a company's response.

What they do not reflect is a genuine desire to understand how any given crisis is likely to be perceived by the stakeholders who matter to the company, and what reasonable people among those stakeholders would appropriately expect a responsible organization or leader to do in such a situation.

One element of deep knowledge is understanding these ten predictable missteps, and then taking action to prevent them.

These ten behaviors are easily recognizable and avoidable, if only there is a mechanism to challenge leaders to think clearly – name the problem and understand consequences – and to take the pain.

Protections Against Charismatic Leaders

In a "Business World" column in *The Wall Street Journal*, columnist Holman Jenkins noted, quite accurately, that "Organizations need defenses against their charismatic leaders. Otherwise such individuals can too readily bully or seduce others into supporting their vainglorious illusions."[144]

Creating mechanisms that challenge leaders is necessary because in the ordinary course of business people are often afraid to speak candidly to superiors or to name the problem in clear terms. As a result, leaders sometimes make decisions based on faulty information.

More commonly subordinates are reluctant to challenge a course of action that may make the boss feel good but that is manifestly a bad idea. A common element of many of the cases presented here – whether Arthur Andersen, the Catholic Church, the *New York Times* – is that a powerful boss dictated a course of action that defied common sense.

This is especially true among CEOs, or their equivalent in the non-corporate world, who are used to getting their way and unaccustomed to push-back from subordinates. Because many create a culture where their word is unchallengeable, they go unchallenged, with predictable consequences.

This is one reason outsiders such as my firm are frequently called into crises. We may have the emotional discipline, deep knowledge, and intellectual rigor needed to move an organization to a resolution. We may understand how different stakeholders tend to behave and what their expectations are likely to be. We may even have strong technical skills. And we can focus totally on the problem.

But as (or more) important, we have the ability to tell the emperor that he has no clothes. As outsiders we can inject a common-sense view that insiders are often unable to do – not because they lack the ability but because either their view has become too institutionalized, or they fear career consequence from second-guessing a powerful boss.

We are free of both of these burdens. And as outsiders we are often in a position to tell the boss unpleasant truths candidly or to ask, apparently naively, about unintended but fully predictable consequences of particular courses of action.

This latter course of action I have found to be particularly effective. When the client (usually the CEO) is dead set on a course of action we are certain is counterproductive, it is often more useful to engage the client in a form of Socratic questioning than merely asserting that we disagree. It can be far more effective to have the CEO discover for him-or-herself that the course of action being advocated will have far more unpleasant consequences than initially considered.

On being presented with a CEO's initial approach to the crisis, we can say, *Yes, that's certainly one option to consider. Let's think through the intended and unintended consequences of doing that. How would your shareholders perceive this? Your employees? Your board of directors? What would regulators be prompted to do when they became aware of this?*

After the CEO names the consequences, we can then ask, *Is that an outcome you can live with? Is there a better outcome we could have in the same situation? What would that outcome be? And what would we need to do in order to assure that outcome?*

Eventually, the CEO comes to recognize that his or her initial idea may be far less desirable than originally thought. But now the CEO can claim appropriate credit for having found a predictably positive solution, and can then direct actions down the chain of command, without being seen to have given in to advisors or staff.

Leaders are therefore well served to have someone in their circle who can tell truth to power without career consequence, whether it's an outside resource or a trusted manager inside the organization.

The examples that illustrate these 10 counterproductive behaviors demonstrate that surviving a crisis is determined more by how a company responds to the crisis rather than by the event itself. If a company is nimble, thoughtful, and quick to take pre-emptive action before a potentially embarrassing or damaging event takes place, it can often prevent the event and the reputational damage altogether.

More important, every organization will at one time or another face an event that causes it discomfort. The companies that recover quickly tend to be those that avoid the missteps and affirmatively deal with issues before they blow up. And whose leaders exhibit mental readiness: emotional discipline, deep knowledge, and intellectual rigor.

It is precisely in this turning point that a company has the opportunity to exercise a maximum impact on the outcome of the crisis: at the point before damage happens.

In all the examples given above we can see how events might have turned out differently.

> If only President Clinton had said on January 25th, 1998 what he was ultimately forced to say on August 17th, 1998. It would have been embarrassing, even humiliating. But I am convinced he would not have been impeached by the House of Representatives and faced a trial in the Senate. And that his legacy would be different than the one he has.

> If only Salomon Brothers had notified regulators in a timely way of the improper trading it discovered, the management team would not have been fired *en masse*, and the firm might have remained a strong and viable franchise.

➤ If only the National Conference of Catholic Bishops had embraced rather than ignored Father Doyle's 1985 report and recommendations, thousands of children might have been spared the harm caused by abusive priests, and the moral authority of the Catholic Church would not have suffered as it has since 2002.

➤ If only Exxon had mobilized all of its resources to address the oil spill in Prince William Sound, we might not remember the spill decades after the fact.

➤ If only Martha Stewart had owned up to her decision to sell ImClone rather than invent a story about a pre-existing agreement to sell at a particular price, she might have remained the head of a strong company, avoided a prison sentence, and be even more powerful and popular today.

One thing all the examples in this chapter have in common is an inattention to the crisis when attention can do the most good: at the turning point.

Companies that take crises seriously do not wait for the situation to become public or to get out of control. Rather, they constantly monitor potential crises – non-routine events that threaten undesired visibility that in turn threaten reputational harm – and bring all appropriate resources to bear when they can do the most good.

Time is an enemy in a crisis. The missteps noted here deprive a company of time, limit the company's options, allow its adversaries or the media to define the situation to the company's disadvantage, and make it much harder to be effective in solving the problem.

Effective crisis managers are attentive to the patterns that these missteps represent, and are quick to engage management to prevent the patterns from playing out.

Chapter 6:

Putting it All Together:

Mental Readiness Summarized

This chapter pulls together the key elements of mental readiness elaborated in each of the prior chapters, providing a single place to find the principles of mental readiness without the various case studies and other commentary that was interspersed in the earlier chapters.

Summary of Chapter 1: Introduction: Mental Readiness

One of the predictable patterns of crisis response is that the severity of the crisis event does not determine whether an organization gets through the crisis successfully. Rather, the timeliness and effectiveness of the response does.

But timeliness and effectiveness are byproducts of mental readiness, a combination of emotional discipline, deep knowledge, and intellectual rigor.

Emotional Discipline: Every crisis takes place in an environment of emotional resonance: of fear, anger, anguish, embarrassment, shame, or panic. Effective leaders are able to control negative emotions and to remain calm. Even a forced calm can help a leader make smart choices by continuing to think clearly despite having a strong emotional stimulus. As Captain Sullenberger noted, when his plane lost power he had a strong physiological reaction, and had to draw on all his training to force calm on the situation. Emotional discipline also allows the leader to see the crisis for what it is, and to avoid the denial that is often a consequence of emotional response to a crisis.

Emotional discipline can be developed through training, through repetition, and through simulations. At Logos Institute we often run leadership teams through high-stress situations to build their ability to keep calm and think clearly.

<u>Deep Knowledge:</u> Deep knowledge starts with understanding the patterns that drive effective and ineffective crisis response, including the reasons certain things work and certain things don't work.

Deep knowledge includes not only what works and what doesn't work, but WHY. And it is the WHY that matters most. The WHY allows a leader to recognize that however a course of action may seem, if it clearly will not work, because it never works, then the leader should not even try.

With that insight leaders can then focus instead on what is likely to work.

Deep knowledge also includes studying particular crises, both effective and ineffective. This allows leaders to learn tough lessons without experiencing the trauma that took place among those who lived the crisis. That way they can give themselves permission to make choices that might otherwise seem risky.

We saw this in the management philosophy that led Pixar to avoid the mistakes of other Silicon Valley companies after initial success, and also to navigate their being bought by a much larger company while maintaining and enhancing their own value and their parent's.

<u>Intellectual Rigor</u>: There is a rigor to effective crisis management that is equivalent to the rigor found in other business processes. But that rigor is often ignored or misapplied.

The rigor begins with clear thinking. The leader is, among other things, a steward of the organization he or she leads. The CEO has a moral duty to think clearly and to put the interests of the organization first, even if it means doing things that are unpleasant or even painful.

Part of intellectual rigor is naming the problem to be solved. Many leaders deny or ignore a problem, or understate the severity of the problem. But if a problem isn't named clearly it will be very difficult to solve the actual problem. Instead resources are spent trying to solve the symptoms of the problem.

Misnaming the problem is counterproductive for two reasons: First, it leaves the fundamental problem unaddressed. Second, it gives management false hope: the illusion that it is managing the crisis, when in fact it is compounding the difficulties.

Intellectual rigor is also about understanding consequences. That means taking the pain: doing what leaders already know they will need to do eventually, but doing it when it can have a positive effect. If it is clear that the only way to maintain trust is to apologize, then apologize quickly and fully. If it is clear that the CEO will need to be fired, fire him or her quickly. A late apology or late dismissal, after public outcry, will seem forced and insincere, and will come only after the loss of trust and other measures of competitive advantage.

While it is understandable that people, even those with a fiduciary duty to shareholders, may wish to avoid embarrassment, unpleasantness, and pain, it is also notable that having the character to own up to one's mistakes can not only prevent greater pain in the future; it can even enhance a company's stature.

Summary of Chapter 2: Crisis Means Choice

The original word from which the English word *crisis* is derived was an ancient Greek word, *krisis* (κρισις). That word meant a decision or choice that a protagonist in a Greek tragedy had to make at a turning point that would determine his or her destiny. And we remember those who chose poorly. We don't remember those who chose wisely. Indeed, a wise choice would not be the topic of a Greek tragedy, the social media of its day.

The same applies in modern crises. We tend to remember those crises where leaders made poor choices. Stakeholders tend not to remember well-handled crises. And that's okay.

The classic on crisis decision-making is Steven Fink's 1986 *Crisis Management: Planning for the Inevitable*. In it Fink describes crises as a turning point, not necessarily a negative event of bad thing. He describes crises as "prodromal" – as precursors or predictors of something yet to come.

I believe that understanding crises in the Greek sense – as a moment of decision or choice in which one's destiny is determined – is the key to effective crisis management.

And as with any other management process, there is a rigor to getting it right.

That rigor includes understanding the problem by asking a sequence of questions intended to help make smart choices:

➤ Question 1: What do we have? Unless we name the problem accurately we will be unable to actually solve the problem quickly. There are several challenges in naming problem. First, there is a tendency to confuse a symptom of a problem for the problem itself (e.g. "We have a *60 Minutes* problem" rather than "We have an inappropriate business practice that is about to become public"). Sometimes the original description of the problem is based on confusion or lack of understanding. Hence, General Motors mischaracterized a safety issue as a customer inconvenience, with fatal consequences.

➤ Question 2: What does it mean? Here we assess the significance of the problem. What are the likely consequences? How are the stakeholders who matter to us likely to react?

➤ Question 3: What do we want? We can't un-ring a bell, but we can consider the less bad outcome among the options available to us.

➤ Question 4: How do we make the less bad outcome happen? How do we consider options and outcomes in such a way that we choose the less bad outcome? Too often leaders in crisis fail to consider options. But there's always more than one way to fix a problem. Or they choose among options based on personal preference or self-protection. When options don't immediately present themselves, we can project options based on magnitudes of response. Option 1: Do nothing out of the ordinary. Option 2: Do something small. Option 3: Do something big.

The most productive way to choose among those options is to consider the options always in connection to the likely outcomes, both intended and unintended, positive and negative.

Sometimes leaders make poor choices because they think that crisis response is just an exercise in public relations. But seeing PR as the solution to a crisis is a recipe for failure.

Every crisis is a business problem before it is a communication problem. Crisis communication is a subset of crisis management that focuses on engaging stakeholders when trust, confidence, and other measures of competitive advantage are at risk.

But communication by itself is rarely enough. Effective crisis response calibrates smart action with smart communication.

Summary of Chapter 3: Decision Criterion #1: What to Do

Crisis management is the management of choices at a turning point where an organization's destiny can go one way or another. Organizations that get through crises well make smart choices at the right time.

But there is often a kind of agony in the decision-making process. The key to getting the decision right is to think clearly. And thinking clearly means using the right decision criteria – the right basis for choice.

Using the right criteria allows a leader and organization to make smart choices in a matter of minutes.

But most leaders apply the wrong criteria because they ask the wrong questions. They ask some version of *What should we do?* or *What should we say?*

The challenge with this kind of question is that it focuses on the **we** – on the entity or leader in question – rather than on what really matters. This leads to saying things that make the leader feel good but that predictably alienate stakeholders. We saw such examples in the cases of both Netflix and BP.

What is needed is a different kind of thinking that begins not with **I/me/we/us** but with **they/them**. And that's because of the way trust works.

One common goal in a crisis is to maintain or enhance the trust of those who matter – shareholders, employees, customers, regulators, etc.

And trust arises when stakeholders' legitimate expectations are met. Trust falls when expectations are unmet.

Because trust is the consequence of fulfilled expectations, the right question to ask when determining the best course of action in a crisis is not *What should we say?* or *What should we do?*

Rather, think of the stakeholders who matter to your organization. Then, with those stakeholders in mind, ask:

What would reasonable people
appropriately expect a responsible organization or leader to do
when facing this kind of situation.

Asking this question is the most important concept in this book; the most important element of mental readiness.

Framing decisions in light of stakeholder expectations leads to smarter choices faster, and maintains stakeholder trust.

For any stakeholder group we can answer this question to a very granular level:

> ➤ To the level of a large universe, such as all employees, or to a small universe, such as only those unionized hourly workers on the second shift of a particular factory.

> ➤ To the level of all regulators or of particular regulators of a single regulatory agency.

> ➤ To the level of all customers or to only those customers who bought a certain product at a certain retailer on a certain day.

There are many ways to identify such expectations. To start, if there are legal or regulatory requirements, reasonable people would appropriately expect a responsible organization or leader to meet those requirements.

Similarly, does the company have a statement of values, a brand promise, or a code of ethics? Reasonable people would appropriately expect a responsible organization to fulfill the promises that it has set, either explicitly or implicitly.

But regardless of the particular expectations, there is a common expectation that applies to all stakeholder groups all the time: In a crisis, all stakeholders expect a responsible leader or organization to care.

To care that something has happened; to care that people need help; to care that something needs to be done.

The single biggest predictor of loss of trust and confidence is the perception that an organization or leader does not care.

So effective crisis response begins with a timely demonstration of caring. And it continues with a persistent demonstration that the organization and its leader continue to care, for as long as the expectation of caring exists.

What it takes to show we care may vary across time, across stakeholder groups, and across forms of crisis. But that we need to show we care does not change.

Showing we care is not sentimental. It is a leadership discipline; part of mental readiness to do what is necessary to protect trust and confidence in a crisis.

Summary of Chapter 4: Decision Criterion #2: When to Do It

When should an organization in crisis show that it cares?

Just as in considering **what to do**, there is a rigor to considering **when to do it**.

There is a first-mover advantage in crisis response: whoever is the first to define three things typically controls stakeholders' interpretation of an event:

> The nature of the crisis itself.

> The organization's motives.

> The organization's actions.

If the organization does not take the first mover advantage, others can define it in unflattering ways.

Silence is often a reflection on of lack of readiness. Sometimes it is deliberate. But silence is the most toxic approach an organization can employ.

There are three central problems with silence in the early phase of a crisis becoming public:

> When stakeholders expect an organization to care, silence is interpreted as indifference – as the absence of caring. And as a result, trust falls. And in the silence, stakeholders tend to interpret the organization's crisis as an integrity lapse, even as the organization may understand the crisis to be a routine operational setback.

> Worse, silence invites the media, social media, critics, and adversaries to seize the first mover advantage and to paint the organization as affirmatively uncaring. So the nature of the crisis gets exaggerated negatively; the company's motives are characterized as unethical or

lacking in integrity; and the company's actions are characterized as too little, too late, or self-protective.

➢ Even worse, if silence continues when there is an expectation of caring, then victims, critics, adversaries, opportunists, the media, social media, and politicians can begin to rally public opinion against the organization. This is when we see calls for boycotts, protests, picketing, petitions, and also calls for investigations, for lawsuits, and for leaders to be fired.

Organizations can find the balance between keeping trust and protecting themselves in future litigation by identifying the categories of things that can be disclosed without acknowledging blame, guilt, or liability. In general, even risk-averse counsel, when pressed, will agree that the following, in whole or in part and properly drafted, would not necessarily increase risks in future litigation:

➢ Acknowledgment: A statement of awareness that something has happened.

➢ Empathy: If there are or may be victims, an expression of empathy or sympathy.

➢ Values: A declaration of the organization's values, such as "our first concern is the safety of our employees…"

➢ Approach: A summary of the kinds of actions taken or to be taken, such as "we are working with first responders and public safety officials, and will continue to do so until all employees are accounted for."

> ➤ <u>Commitment</u>: Setting future expectations, such as "we will continue to monitor the situation and will provide a public update when we know more."

In our experience, a stand-by statement with those categories is sufficient to secure the first-mover advantage and demonstrate that the organization cares, without triggering undue legal liability.

Of course, the best way to control the communication agenda is through the first mover advantage: Be the first to fully define the crisis, your motive, and your actions.

But what if that's not possible? If something happens unexpectedly? Or if others start talking about you before you're ready? Then there's a need to be nimble.

In these circumstances, it's important to understand the Golden Hour of Crisis Response.

The Golden Hour doesn't refer to a particular number of minutes but rather the observation that incremental delays in controlling the communication agenda lead to greater-than-incremental harm.

The longer it takes to show we care, the harder it becomes. We saw this in the example of United Airlines.

That's because more and more people are reaching conclusions about the situation, making judgments, and believing and acting on what they hear. What would have been sufficient in the early phases of a situation becoming public would be woefully inadequate hours or days or weeks later.

As United Airlines learned, it is much harder to restore trust that has been lost than to preserve it in the first place.

The general principle in applying the Golden Hour in a crisis is the rule of 45 minutes, six hours, three days, two weeks. That's the sequence of disproportionate effects that arise in particular intervals in the cycle of visibility—what used to be called the "news cycle" but with the ubiquity of social media is now far more widespread. This principle suggests that it's possible to show we care, but that the longer it takes to organize a sufficiently persuasive response, the harder it becomes.

If an organization can effectively define the nature of the crisis, its motives, and its actions within the first 45 minutes of an issue becoming public from some external source, relatively few stakeholders will have heard of the issue from others, and things are likely to settle down with minimal harm to trust and likely no long-term harm. Very often, a stand-by statement with the categories noted above is enough to show care quickly, even after losing the first mover advantage.

But if an organization misses the first 45 minutes more and more people will hear about the issue, with critics, adversaries, commentators, and others defining the crisis, the organization's motives, and its actions. It is still possible to take back control of the communication, but it will be harder: the organization will need to reach more people, and overcome more competition for attention. And some people may have already formed opinions that will be very hard to change. But if it can be done within the first six hours of the issue becoming public, then things should settle down relatively quickly. As in the first-mover advantage and in the first 45 minutes, a well-crafted standby statement may be sufficient to show care in the first six hours. But stakeholder expectations may require that the organization provide more detail about the actions taken so far.

If it takes more than several hours to define the crisis, motives, and actions, then a company and its leaders will be at risk for three days. That's because of the dynamics of daily newspaper publication and television news broadcasts, along with television and social media reaction to the initial story or stories, and any second-day newspaper stories and subsequent reaction. During this period, even more people are being made aware of the issue by critics, the media, or others. And the company and its leaders are more and more at risk. It is typically within this window that victims, opportunists, activists, critics, and media begin to call for boycotts, petitions, firings, investigations, and lawsuits. But if within three days the organization can show it cares, the situation should resolve itself. But what it takes to show it cares is much more difficult on the third day than in the first 45 minutes or six hours.

If it takes more than several days for a company or its leaders to define the crisis, its motives, and its actions, then significantly more people will know about the crisis, and it will be even harder to resolve the it. And because of the publication schedule of weekly magazines, weekly newspaper sections, weekly blogs, and television programs, the likelihood is that a controversy will be alive for at least two weeks.

If it takes more than two weeks to define the issue, motives, and actions, then there's a very good chance of significant damage, sometimes irreparable. We saw that with Tony Hayward and BP: He became untenable as CEO and had to leave the company.

Just as with the decision criteria for What, the criteria for deciding When to show care are based on stakeholders' expectations and their likely reactions. And as with the criteria for What, the key is to ask the right questions. We have found that four questions in particular are most productive. A Yes answer to any one of them is sufficient to give an organization and its leadership confidence that engaging stakeholders is a wise move.

The four questions are these:

1. Will those who matter to us expect us to do or say something now?

2. Will silence be seen by our stakeholders as indifference or as an affirmation of guilt?

3. Are others talking about us now, thereby shaping the perception of us among those who matter to us; is there reason to believe they will be soon?

4. If we wait do we lose the ability to determine the outcome?

If the answer to all four questions is No, then we have an opportunity to monitor and to prepare, to rehearse, to draft documents, to secure approvals, and otherwise get ready to engage. Then, when the answer to any one of the questions becomes Yes, we can engage effectively. And we'll have either the first mover advantage or respond sufficiently quickly within the Golden Hour that there will be minimal loss of trust.

Summary of Chapter 5: Consequences of Lack of Mental Readiness: 10 Common Crisis Missteps

Deep knowledge allows leaders to learn tough lessons without living those lessons directly. They do this by, among other things, studying the predictable patterns that play out in crises, including the patterns of missteps.

In the late 1980s I began noticing a pattern in crisis missteps that companies and organizations commonly make, and have kept an inventory of them ever since. At the Logos Institute for Crisis Management and Executive Leadership we continue to maintain and build upon that inventory.

What is remarkable is that the pattern of missteps has not changed over the 30 years that I have been actively working on crises, even as technology, social media, and social norms have changed.

I have witnessed these missteps in organizations operating on six continents. They serve as a kind of common denominator in institutional responses to negative events.

Enlightened institutions and their advisors are on guard against these behaviors, and act promptly to overcome them if they arise. Anyone in a position to help handle crisis response, whether from within an organization or as an outside advisor, should be alert to signs of any of these behaviors.

The ten counterproductive behaviors are:

1. Ignore the problem

2. Deny the severity of the problem

3. Compartmentalize the problem

4. Tell misleading half-truths

5. Lie

6. Tell only part of the story; let the story dribble out

7. Assign blame

8. Over-confess

9. Panic and paralysis

10. Shoot the messenger

As noted in Chapter 1, the best leaders have a mix of humility and resolve, allowing them to seek help and to take advice. But often leaders' charisma overtakes humility. One common element of the missteps identified in this chapter is that they tend to take place when powerful leaders inhibit candid discussion of problems, which can be deadly in a crisis.

In those instances, creating internal structures or soliciting outside advice to challenge leaders is necessary because some people are afraid to speak candidly to superiors or to name the problem in clear terms. More commonly subordinates are reluctant to challenge a course of action that may make the boss feel good but that is manifestly a bad idea, for fear of retaliation. This is especially true among CEOs, and their equivalent in the non-corporate world, who are used to getting their way and unaccustomed to push-back from subordinates. Because many create a culture where their word is unchallengeable, they go unchallenged, with predictable negative consequences.

This is one reason outsiders such as my firm are frequently called into crises. We have the ability to tell the emperor that he has no clothes. As outsiders, we can inject a common-sense view that insiders are often unable to do – not because they lack the ability but because their view has become too institutionalized or they fear career consequence from second-guessing a powerful boss.

We are free of both of these burdens. And as outsiders we are often in a position to tell the boss unpleasant truths candidly or to ask, apparently naively, about unintended but fully predictable consequences of particular courses of action, and to guide them toward alternatives.

Closing Thoughts

One of the burdens leaders face is the need to protect the enterprise value of their organizations. This includes, among other things, being effective stewards of reputation, of stakeholders' trust and confidence in the organization and its leaders, and of other tangible and intangible assets – such as stock price, competitive position, and employee productivity – that are driven by reputation, trust, and confidence.

This book is one path toward effective stewardship. It is a testament to the power of Deep Knowledge, the inventory of patterns and cases that help leaders understand what works, what doesn't work

– and in particular WHY something works or doesn't work – in a crisis.

Understanding the patterns and the particular cases, both positive and negative, gives leaders a competitive advantage in navigating crises effectively. This understanding combined with Emotional Discipline and Intellectual Rigor constitute Mental Readiness, which allows leaders to make smart choices when the leader has maximum control of the outcome, in the turning point moment when a company's destiny is set one way or the other.

Beyond Mental Readiness, organizations are well served to also have Operational Readiness: structures, systems, protocols, that allow companies to know anticipate what could go wrong, mitigate where possible, and execute effective crisis response when necessary. Operational readiness will be the subject of a future Logos Institute best practices guide.

In the meantime, we hope you find this volume, on mental readiness, useful and empowering.

About the Author

For more than 35 years Helio Fred Garcia has helped leaders build trust, inspire loyalty, and lead effectively. He is a coach, counselor, teacher, writer, and speaker whose clients include some of the largest and best-known companies and organizations in the world.

Fred is president of the crisis management firm Logos Consulting Group and executive director of the Logos Institute for Crisis Management & Executive Leadership. He is based in New York and has worked with clients in dozens of countries on six continents.

Fred has 38 years of experience counseling securities firms, banks, insurance companies, specialized financial and professional service firms, corporations, not-for-profits, and governments. He has particular expertise in crisis, change, and risk management; crisis communication; international security issues; international financial transactions; corporate governance; business ethics; and executive leadership.

Fred has coached more than 400 CEOs of major corporations, plus thousands of other high-profile people in other complex fields, including doctors, scientists, lawyers, financial executives, military officers, and government officials. These executives, on six continents, were in industries as diverse as pharmaceuticals, energy, heavy manufacturing, biotechnology, computer software, financial services, law firms, advertising agencies, religious denominations, armed forces, universities, and not-for-profit advocacy groups. In the 1980s he worked at leading public relations firms and served as head of public relations for a global investment bank and for a large public accounting firm. Through the 1990s Fred headed the crisis practice of a leading strategic communication consulting firm.

Fred is a highly sought keynote and motivational speaker. He has keynoted major conferences and events in the United States, South America, Europe, Africa, the Middle East, and Asia. Fred speaks about crisis management, leadership communication, business ethics, journalist/source relationships, and ways to maintain trust in difficult situations.

Fred has been on the New York University faculty since 1988. He is an adjunct professor of management in NYU's Stern School of Business Executive MBA program, where he teaches crisis management, and where in 2016 he was named an Executive MBA Great Professor.

He is an adjunct associate professor of management and communication in NYU's School of Professional Studies, MS in Public Relations and Corporate Communication, program, where he received the Dean's awards for teaching excellence in 1990 and 2017. He also received awards for outstanding service and for 25 years service in teaching. In that program he teaches courses in communication strategy; in communication ethics, law, and regulation; and in crisis communication.

Fred is also an adjunct associate professor at Columbia University, where he teaches ethics in the Fu Foundation School of Engineering and Applied Science.

Fred is a Senior Fellow in the Institute of Corporate Communication at Communication University of China in Beijing. For eight years until 2015 Fred served on the leadership faculty of the Center for Security Studies of the Swiss Federal Institute of Technology (ETH), Zurich, Switzerland, where he taught an intensive seminar in the Master's in Advanced Studies in Crisis Management and Security Policy.

He has also served on the adjunct faculty of the Starr King School for the Ministry -- Graduate Theological Union in Berkeley, CA, where for six years he taught a seminar on religious leadership for social change. He is a frequent guest lecturer at the Wharton School of Business of the University of Pennsylvania, U.S. Defense Information School, the U.S. Marine Corps Command and Staff College, U.S. Marine Corps Officer Candidate School, the Brookings Institution, and at other universities around the world.

Fred is author of *The Power of Communication: Skills to Build Trust, Inspire Loyalty, and Lead Effectively*, FT Press, 2012. That book was on the United States Marine Corps Commandant's Professional Reading List from 2013 to 2017. It was published in Chinese in 2014 by Pearson Education Asia Ltd. in Hong Kong and Publishing House of Electronics Industry in Beijing.

In addition to The *Power of Communication* and its two companion videos (*Nine Principles of Effective Leadership Communication* and *The Physicality of Audience Engagement*, FT Press, 2012), Fred is co-author (with John Doorley) of *Reputation Management: The Key to Successful Public Relations and Corporate Communication*, third edition 2015; second edition 2011; first edition 2007 by Routledge, Taylor & Francis Group; Korean language edition 2016 by Alma Books, Seoul, Republic of Korea; Chinese translation pending, 2017; French translation pending, 2017. His two-volume book *Crisis Communications* was published by AAAA Publications in 1999.

Fred is accredited by the Public Relations Society of America, and received the Society's New York Chapter's Philip Dorf Award for mentoring.

Fred has an MA in philosophy from Columbia University and two graduate certificates in classical Greek language and literature from the Latin/Greek Institute of the City University of New York Graduate Center. He has a BA with honors in politics and philosophy from New York University, where he was named a University Honors Scholar and was elected to Phi Beta Kappa. He received an honorary doctorate in Humane Letters from Mount Saint Mary College.

Notes

[1] *The 18 Immutable Laws of Corporate Reputation: Creating, Protecting, and Repairing Your Most Valuable Asset,* by Ronald J. Alsop, Wall Street Journal Books, 2004, page 218.

[2] Secrets of Leadership from American Express: The Key to Ken Chenault's Plan for American Express: Industrial-Strength Candor," by Geoff Colvin, *Fortune,* October 1, 2007. http://money.cnn.com/2007/09/17/news/newsmakers/Ken_Chenault.fortune/index.htm

[3] "Secrets of Leadership from American Express: The Key to Ken Chenault's Plan for American Express: Industrial-Strength Candor," Ibid.

[4] "The Five Stages of Crisis Management" by Jack Welch, *The Wall Street Journal,* September 12, 2005, page A20.

[5] Jack Welch, The Wall Street Journal, Ibid.

[6] "Secrets of Leadership from American Express: The Key to Ken Chenault's Plan for American Express: Industrial-Strength Candor," Ibid.

[7] CBS Sixty Minutes, February 8, 2009.

[8] Personal testimonial by Logos Institute client.

[9] "Level 5 Leadership: the Triumph of Humility and Fierce Resolve, by Jim Collins, *Harvard Business Review,* July-August, 2005, at https://hbr.org/2005/07/level-5-leadership-the-triumph-of-humility-and-fierce-resolve

[10] "What Makes a Good Leader?" by Daniel Goleman, *Harvard Business Review,* January, 2004, at https://hbr.org/2004/01/what-makes-a-leader

[11] Jim Collins, Ibid.

[12] His Holiness Pope Francis, Ted Talk, transcript translated by Elena Montrasio, at https://www.ted.com/talks/pope_francis_why_the_only_future_worth_building_includes_everyone/transcript?language=en

[13] His Holiness Pope Francis, Ted Talk, Ibid.

[14] *Strifeblog,* a publication of the Department of War Studies, King's College London, http://www.strifeblog.org/2013/05/07/with-rifle-and-bibliography-general-mattis-on-professional-reading/

[15] Catmull, Ed, *Creativity, Inc.* (New York: Random House, 2014), XIV.

[16] Catmull, *Creativity, Inc.*, Ibid., XIV.

[17] Catmull, *Creativity, Inc.*, Ibid., 220

[18] Catmull, *Creativity, Inc.*, Ibid., 220.

[19] Catmull, *Creativity, Inc.*, Ibid., 93.

[20] Catmull, *Creativity, Inc.*, Ibid., 245.

[21] Catmull, *Creativity, Inc.*, Ibid., 247.

[22] Catmull, *Creativity, Inc.*, Ibid., 261.

[23] Catmull, *Creativity, Inc.*, Ibid., 258.

[24] Catmull, *Creativity, Inc.*, Ibid., 249.

[25] Michael Novak, *The Spirit of Democratic Capitalism*, Latham, 1982.

[26] Matthew L. Wald and Danielle Ivory, "G.M. Is Fined Over Safety and Called a Lawbreaker," The New York Times, May 16, 2014, at http://www.nytimes.com/2014/05/17/business/us-fines-general-motors-35-million-for-lapses-on-ignition-switch-defect.html

[27] Report to the Board of Directors of General Motors Company Regarding Switch Recalls, by Anton R. Valukas, Jenner & Block, May 29, 2014, pages 1-2.

[28] Valukas report, page 2

[29] Valukas report, pages 2-3

[30] Announcement by the United States Department of Justice, Southern District of New York, September 17, 2015, at https://www.justice.gov/usao-sdny/pr/manhattan-us-attorney-announces-criminal-charges-against-general-motors-and-deferred

[31] In this case, as in all others involving unnamed clients, several identifying details have been withheld or adapted to protect their identities. We are contractually forbidden from disclosing who they are. But none of the modifications changes the dynamics of what happened or lessons learned.

[32] "Corporate Mea Culpas Shown to Pay" by Jane J. Kim, *The Wall Street Journal*, April 21, 2004, page B4D.

[33] All Greek translations from *A Lexicon Abridged from Liddell and Scott's Greek-English Lexicon*, Oxford At The Clarendon Press, 1989, page 394

[34] *Crisis Management: Planning for the Inevitable*, by Steven Fink, American Management Association, 1986, p. 15.

[35] Fink, Ibid., pp. 15-16.

[36] Fink, Ibid., p. 16.

[37] Scene from *Butch Cassidy and the Sundance Kid*, 1969, at https://www.youtube.com/watch?v=ck6vqsOt-Pc

[38] *Butch Cassidy and the Sundance Kid*, Ibid.

[39] http://flavell.mit.edu/2017/04/26/hour-solve-problem-life-depended-solution-spend-first-55-minutes-determining-proper-question-ask-know-proper-question-coul/

[40] *Improvised News; A Sociological Study of Rumor*, by Tamotsu Shibutani, Bobbs Merrill, 1966, page 172. Note: Shibutani uses the gender-specific words "man" or "men" to refer to people in general. Throughout, I will quote him using the gender-neutral "person" or "people."

[41] "We Can't Solve Problems By Using the Same Kind of Thinking We Used When We Created Them, by David Mielach, BusinessNewsDaily, April 19, 2012, at http://www.businessinsider.com/we-cant-solve-problems-by-using-the-same-kind-of-thinking-we-used-when-we-created-them-2012-4

[42] Jessie Becker, "Netflix Introduces New Plans and Announces Price Changes," Web log post, *The Netflix Blog*. Netflix Inc., 12 July 2011, at http://blog.netflix.com/2011/07/netflix-introduces-new-plans-and.html.

[43] Becker "Netflix," Ibid.

[44] Becker "Netflix," Ibid.

[45] Becker "Netflix," Ibid.

[46] Reed Hastings, "An Explanation and Some Reflections," Web log post, *The Netflix Blog*, Netflix Inc., 18 Sept. 2011, at http://blog.netflix.com/2011/09/explanation-and-some-reflections.html.

[47] Hastings, "An Explanation," Ibid.

[48] Hastings, "An Explanation," Ibid.

[49] Hastings, "An Explanation," Ibid.

[50] Hastings, "An Explanation," Ibid.

[51] Patrick Seitz, "Netflix Tries Damage Control; Qwikster Doesn't Help," *Investor's Business Daily*, Investor's Business Daily, Inc., 19 Sept. 2011, at http://news.investors.com/Article/585222/201109191639/Netflix-Apologizes-To-Customers-Then-Angers-Them.htm.

[52] David Pogue, "Parsing Netflix's 'Apology,'" *The New York Times*, 22 Sept. 2011, at http://pogue.blogs.nytimes.com/2011/09/22/parsing-netflixs-apology/.

[53] Pogue, "Parsing," Ibid.

[54] Pogue, "Parsing," Ibid.

[55] Pogue, "Parsing," Ibid.

[56] Reed Hastings, "DVDs Will Be Staying at Netflix.com," Web log post, *The Netflix Blog*, Netflix Inc., 10 Oct. 2011, at http://blog.netflix.com/2011/10/dvds-will-be-staying-at-netflixcom.html

[57] Hastings, "DVDs," Ibid.

[58] Frank J. Narvan, "If "Trust Leads to Loyalty" What Leads to Trust?" *Ethics Resource Center*, 1996, Web. <http://www.ethics.org/resources/articles-organizational-ethics.a>.

[59] https://www.ftc.gov/public-statements/1983/10/ftc-policy-statement-deception

[60] James E. Lukaszewski, *Lukaszewski on Crisis Communication: What Your CEO Needs to Know About Reputation Risk and Crisis Management*, Rothstein Associates Inc.; First Edition (March 11, 2013), page 23.

[61] Lukaszewski, page 25.

[62] BBC interview with Tony Hayward, November 9, 2010, https://www.youtube.com/watch?v=bwRiUx5t664

[63] United States Coast Guard. *On Scene Coordinator Report Deepwater Horizon Oil Spill*. Rep. Washington, D.C.: United States Coast Guard, 2011: 33.

[64] Krauss, Clifford. "Oil Spill's Blow to BP's Image May Eclipse Costs." *The New York Times*. The New York Times, 29 Apr. 2010. Web. <http://www.nytimes.com/2010/04/30/business/30bp.html>.

[65] "BP Vows to Clean up Gulf of Mexico Oil Slick." *BBC News*. BBC, 03 Mar. 2010. Web. <http://news.bbc.co.uk/2/hi/americas/8658081.stm>.

[66] Webb, Tim. "BP Boss Admits Job on the Line over Gulf Oil Spill." *The Guardian*. Guardian News and Media Limited, 13 May 2010. Web. <http://www.theguardian.com/business/2010/may/13/bp-boss-admits-mistakes-gulf-oil-spill>.

[67] "BP CEO On Need To Stop Oil Spill: 'I Would Like My Life Back'" *YouTube*. YouTube, 31 May 2010. Web. <http://www.youtube.com/watch?v=EIA_sL4cSlo>.

[68] "Exerts: BP ignored warning signs on doomed well," by Dana Capiello, Associated Press http://www.seattletimes.com/business/experts-bp-ignored-warning-signs-on-doomed-well/

[69] "Report Faults BP and Contractors in Rig Explosion and Spill," by John M. Broder, The New York Times, November 17, 2010, http://www.nytimes.com/2010/11/18/us/18BP.html?hp

[70] "Lawmakers accuse BP of 'shortcuts'" by Steven Mufson and Anne E. Kornblut, *Washington Post*, June 15, 2010, page A1, at http://www.washingtonpost.com/wp-dyn/content/article/2010/06/14/AR2010061403580_pf.html

[71] "Lawmakers accuse BP of 'shortcuts,'" *Washington Post*, ibid.

[72] "BP's Spill Contingency Plans Vastly Inadequate, CBS News, June 9, 2010, at http://www.cbsnews.com/news/bps-spill-contingency-plans-vastly-inadequate/

[73] https://www.theguardian.com/world/video/2013/jun/13/australia-army-chief-women-video

[74] Australia Army Chief Video, Ibid.

[75] Australia Army Chief Video, Ibid.

[76] Australia Army Chief Video, Ibid.

[77] "'Jedi Council' sex ring: 171 Australian Defense Force staff disciplined," *The Guardian*, August 7, 2014, https://www.theguardian.com/world/2014/aug/07/jedi-council-sex-ring-171-australian-defence-force-staff-disciplined

[78] "David Morrison, former chief of army, named Australian of the Year," *The Guardian*, https://www.theguardian.com/australia-news/2016/jan/25/david-morrison-former-chief-of-army-named-australian-of-the-year

[79] James E. Lukaszewski, Lukaszewski on Crisis Communication: What Your CEO Needs to Know About Reputation, Risk, and Crisis Management," Rothstein Associates, 2013, pp 13-14.

[80] Alsop, Ibid., 218.

[81] James E. Lukasewski, personal letter to the author, April 15, 2017.

[82] Lukasewski, personal letter, Ibid.

[83] Lukasewski, personal letter, Ibid.

[84] *The 18 Immutable Laws of Corporate Reputation: Creating, Protecting, and Repairing Your Most Valuable Asset*, by Ronald J. Alsop, A Wall Street Journal Book, Free Press, 2004, page 220.

[85] Australia Army Chief Video, Ibid.

[86] Tweet by United Airlines, April 10, 2017.

[87] Tweet by Maryrose @MaryroseBisagna, April 10, 2017.

[88] "Jimmy Kimmel rips United with fake ad after passenger dragged off plane" by Erin Jensen, *USAToday*, at https://www.usatoday.com/story/life/entertainthis/2017/04/11/jimmy-kimmel-rips-united-creates-fake-ad-after-customer-is-dragged-from-seat/100316622/

[89] "Read the full text of United CEO's Controversial Letter to Employees" by Alana Horowitz Satlin, *Huffington Post*, April 11, 2017, at http://www.huffingtonpost.com/entry/united-ceo-letter-employees_us_58ec9516e4b0c89f9120edc0

[90] "Read the full text of United CEO's Controversial Letter to Employees," *Huffington Post*, Ibid.

[91] United Airlines company statement, at https://hub.united.com/united-express-3411-statement-oscar-munoz-2355968629.html

[92] "United CEO feels 'shame,' passengers will be compensated," *ABC News*, at http://abcnews.go.com/US/united-ceo-oscar-munoz-felt-sham-passenger-dragged/story?id=46746594

[93] "United CEO feels 'shame,' passengers will be compensated," *ABC News*, Ibid.

[94] "United CEO feels 'shame,' passengers will be compensated," *ABC News*, Ibid.

[95] "United CEO feels 'shame,' passengers will be compensated," *ABC News*, Ibid.

[96] "United CEO feels 'shame,' passengers will be compensated," *ABC News*, Ibid.

[97] "United CEO feels 'shame,' passengers will be compensated," *ABC News*, Ibid.

[98] "See Melissa McCarthy's Sean Spicer Apologize for Hitler Remark on 'SNL'" by Daniel Kreps, *Rolling Stone*, April 16, 2017, at http://www.rollingstone.com/tv/news/see-melissa-mccarthys-sean-spicer-apologize-on-snl-w477042

[99] "United CEO Oscar Munoz will not become chairman next year as planned," by Danielle Muoio, *Business Insider*, April 21, 2017, at http://www.rollingstone.com/tv/news/see-melissa-mccarthys-sean-spicer-apologize-on-snl-w477042

[100] *United Express Flight 3411 Review and Action Report*, United Airlines, April 27, 2017, downloadable at http://uafly.co/scmf/OrMCe04Lcp0lOLk3ezw_qxQK2TYEP0NPE HFHT56-xqmU6D_KfjlBKBEOR036Q5fJJfu2r5of5VHHupa_BGwtnUw0mil2 C3Kd/ReviewActionReport

[101] ""I'm Too Pretty to Do Homework" T-shirt Yanked," *CBS News*, CBS Interactive Inc., 1 Sept. 2011, Web,

http://www.cbsnews.com/stories/2011/09/01/earlyshow/living/pare
nting/main20100427.shtml.

[102] Mark Tatge, "Can Bell Ring In New McDonald's?" *Forbes*, 19 Apr. 2004, at http://www.forbes.com/2004/04/19/cz_mt_0419mcd2.html.

[103] Tatge, "Can Bell Ring In New McDonald's?" Ibid.

[104] Carol Hymowitz and Joann S. Lublin, "McDonald's CEO Tragedy Holds Lessons for Directors," *The Wall Street Journal*, 20 Apr. 2004, at <http://online.wsj.com/article/0,,SB1082417091192287202,00.html>.

[105] Hymowitz and Lublin "McDonald's," Ibid.

[106] Hymowitz and Lublin "McDonald's," Ibid.

[107] Hymowitz and Lublin "McDonald's," Ibid.

[108] Melanie Warner and Patrick McGeehan, "Change at Helm, but a Steady Course at McDonald's," *The New York Times*, 24 Nov. 2004, at http://www.nytimes.com/2004/11/24/business/24burger.html.

[109] Jukaszewski, personal letter, Ibid.

[110] To protect client confidentiality, in a very few cases in this chapter I change one or two identifying features of the un-named company being discussed. At no time do I change the circumstances of the crisis. Some of the named companies have been clients, but here I draw only on the public record, and do not disclose any information given in confidence. And I do not disclose that they were clients.

[111] "Blame Congress, Not NHTSA" by Adam Zagorin, Time, September 18, 2000, at http://www.time.com/time/archive/preview/0,10987,1101000918-54419,00.html

[112] *Final Accounting: Ambition, Greed, and the Fall of Arthur Andersen*, by Barbara Ley Toffler with Jennifer Reingold, Broadway Books, 2003, page 7.

[113] *Final Accounting*, Ibid., page 124.

[114] *Final Accounting*, Ibid., pages 124 to 126.

[115] *Final Accounting*, Ibid., page 60.

[116] *Final Accounting*, Ibid., page 8.

[117] Press release by Massachusetts Attorney General, July 23, 2003, at http://www.ago.state.ma.us/press_rel/archreport.asp?searchStr=1 See also *The Sexual Abuse of Children in the Roman Catholic Archdiocese of Boston: A Report by the Attorney General*, Office of the Attorney General, Commonwealth of Massachusetts, July 23, 2003, at http://www.ago.state.ma.us/press_rel/archreport.asp?searchStr=1.

[118] http://www.boston.com/globe/spotlight/abuse/extras/bishops_map.htm

[119] "A Short History of the 'Manual'" by Thomas Doyle, OP, JCD, pages 4 and 5, athttp://www.snapnetwork.org/doyle_reports/history_of_1985_manual.htm

[120] *The Problem of Sexual Molestation by Roman Catholic Clergy, Meeting the Problem in a Comprehensive and Responsible Manner*, Report to the National Conference of Catholic Bishops, 1985, by F. Ray Mouton, Rev. Michael Peterson, and Rev. Thomas P. Doyle, pages 5-6.

[121] *The Problem of Sexual Molestation by Roman Catholic Clergy*, Ibid., page 90.

[122] "A Short History of the 'Manual'" by Thomas Doyle, Ibid., page 5.

[123] http://www.boston.com/globe/spotlight/abuse/cost/

[124] "The Catholic Church Crisis Revisited," *Voice of Reason*, No. 1, 2003, page 3.

[125] "Santa Fe archdiocese learned lessons that could help others; How the church survived 'our dark night of the soul'" by Marco R. della Cava, *USA Today*, March 26, 2002, page 1.

[126] "Santa Fe archdiocese learned lessons that could help others; How the church survived 'our dark night of the soul'" Ibid.

[127] *Liar's Poker* by Michael Lewis, Penguin, 1990, page 34.

[128] "The Salomon Shocker: How Bad Will It Get?" by Gary Weiss, Leah Nathans-Spiro, and Jeffrey M. Laderman with Michel MacNamee and Dean Fouts, *Business Week*, August 21, 1991, at http://www.businessweek.com/@@3t1TboUQdQ5ltAAA/archives/1991/b322846.arc.htm

[129] "Salomon Shocker," *Business Week*, Ibid.

[130] http://www.jnj.com/our_company/awards/index.htm

[131] "AMR board pressured as unions set new votes, Statement needed on perks: Experts" by Ameet Sachdev, April 23, 2003, at http://www.chicagotribune.com/business/chi-0304230265apr23,1,7701910.story

[132] "Bridgestone/Firestone Announces Recall" by James R. Healey and Sara Nathan, *USA Today*, August 10, 2000, at http://www.usatoday.com/money/consumer/autos/mauto730.htm.

[133] Testimony of Bridgestone/Firestone, Inc. Before the Senate Commerce Committee, September 12, 2000, page 5, at

http://216.239.39.104/search?q=cache:tuPAWv0YE_IJ:www.senate.g ov/~commerce/hearings/0912fir.pdf+%22Bridgestone/Firestone%22 +and+%22recall%22+and+%22timing%22&hl=en&ie=UTF-8

[134] "Times Reporter Who Resigned Leaves Long Trail of Deception" reported and written by Dan Barry, David Barstow, Jonathan D. Glater, Adam Liptak and Jacques Steinberg research support provided by Alain Delaquérière and Carolyn Wilder, *The New York Times*, May 11, page 1.

[135] "Editor of Times Tells Staff He Accepts Blame for Fraud" by Jacques Sternberg, *The New York Times*, May 15, 2003, page 1.

[136] "My Times" by Howell Raines, *The Atlantic*, May, 2004, page 75.

[137] Raines, ibid, page 78,

[138] Raines, Ibid., page 75.

[139] Interview by President Clinton with Jim Lehrer, *The Newshour with Jim Lehrer*, PBS, January 21, 1998.

[140] Chronology for the Martha Stewart trial is derived from MSNBC website: http://www.msnbc.msn.com/id/4429271/, March 6, 2004.

[141] Unsigned editorial, "Mayhem Over Martha," *The Wall Street, Journal*, June 5, 2003, page A16.

[142] "NYSE's a Tough Market for Press: Reporters Are Watched as They Get Brief Glimpse of Grasso Pay Documents" by Matthew Rose, *The Wall Street Journal*, September 11, 2003, at http://online.wsj.com/PA2VJBNA4R/article/0,,SB106323318334075 000-search,00.html

[143] "NYSE's a Tough Market for Press: Reporters Are Watched as They Get Brief Glimpse of Grasso Pay Documents" by Matthew Rose, *The Wall Street Journal*, Ibid.

[144] "Business World" column by Holman Jenkins, *The Wall Street Journal*, August 19, 1998, p. A19.

Made in the USA
Middletown, DE
14 July 2017